CONTENTS

Note. In the following Rules the words **MUST/ MUST NOT** refer to the requirements of the law.

GENERAL

1. Where there is a pavement or footpath, use it. Where possible, avoid walking next to the kerb with your back to the traffic. If you have to step into the road, watch out for traffic.

2. Where there is no pavement or footpath, walk on the right-hand side of the road so that you can see oncoming traffic. Keep close to the side of the road. Take care at sharp right-hand bends; it may be safer to cross the road well before you reach one so that oncoming traffic has a better chance of seeing you. After the bend cross back to face the oncoming traffic. Walk in single file if possible, especially on narrow roads or in poor light.

Be seen in the dark – wear something reflective.

3. Wear or carry something that will help you to be seen. Light-coloured, bright or fluorescent items will help in poor visibility. At night use reflective materials (eg reflective armbands and sashes) which can be seen in headlights up to three times as far away as non-reflective materials.

4. Do not let young children out alone on the pavement or road (see Rule 7). When taking children out, walk between them and the traffic and hold their hands firmly. Strap very young children in push-chairs or use reins.

5. A group of people involved in an organised march on the road should keep to the left. There should be look-outs in front and at the back wearing fluorescent clothes in daylight and reflective clothes in the dark. At night, the look-out in front should carry a white light and the one at the back a bright red light which is visible from behind. People on the outside of large groups should also carry lights and wear reflective clothing.

6. You **MUST NOT** walk on motorways or their slip roads except in an emergency (see Rule 183).

CROSSING THE ROAD

The Green Cross Code
7. The Green Cross Code gives advice on crossing the road. It is for all pedestrians. Children should be taught it and should not be allowed out alone until they can understand and use it properly. The age when they can do this is different for each child. Many children under ten cannot judge how fast vehicles are going or how far away they are. Children learn by example, so parents should always use the Code in full when out with children. Parents are responsible for deciding at what age their children can use it safely by themselves.

a First find a safe place to cross, then stop.
It is safer to cross at subways, footbridges, islands, Zebra, Pelican and Puffin crossings, traffic lights or where there is a police officer, school crossing patrol or traffic warden. Otherwise choose a place where you can see clearly in all directions. Try to avoid crossing between parked cars (see Rule 23). Move to a space where drivers can see you clearly.

b Stand on the pavement near the kerb.
Stop just before you get to the kerb – where you can see if anything is coming, but where you will not be too close to the traffic. If there is no pavement, stand back from the edge of the road but make sure you can still see approaching traffic.

c Look all around for traffic and listen.
Traffic could come from any direction, so look along every road. Listen also because you can sometimes hear traffic before you see it.

d If traffic is coming, let it pass. Look all around again.
If there is any traffic near, let it go past. Then look around again. Listen to make sure no other traffic is coming.

e When there is no traffic near, walk straight across the road.
When there is no traffic near, it is safe to cross. Remember, even if traffic is a long way off, it may be approaching very quickly.

When it is safe, walk straight across the road – do not run.

f Keep looking and listening for traffic while you cross.
When you have started to cross, keep looking and listening in case there is any traffic you did not see – or in case other traffic suddenly appears.

Crossing where there is a central island in the road

8. Use the Green Cross Code to cross to the island. Stop there and use the Code again to cross the second half of the road.

Crossing at a junction

9. When you cross the road at a junction look out for traffic coming round the corner, especially from behind you.

Crossing at a Zebra crossing

10. If there is a Zebra crossing nearby, use it. Do not cross at the side of a crossing on the zig-zag lines – it is very dangerous.

11. Give traffic plenty of time to see you and to stop before you start to cross. Vehicles need more time to stop when rain or ice have made the road slippery. If necessary put one foot on the crossing; until you have stepped on to a Zebra crossing, the traffic does not have to stop. But do not cross until the traffic has stopped. Do not push a wheelchair or pram on to the crossing until the traffic has stopped.

12. When the traffic has stopped, walk straight across but keep looking both ways and listening in case a driver or rider has not seen you and attempts to overtake a vehicle that has stopped.

13. If there is an island in the middle of a crossing, wait on the island and follow Rules 11 and 12 before you cross the second half of the road – it is a separate crossing.

Crossing at a Pelican crossing

14. If there is a Pelican crossing nearby, use it. Do not cross at the side of a crossing on the zig-zag lines – it is very dangerous. At this type of crossing the traffic lights instruct the traffic when to stop and pedestrians when to cross. When the red figure shows, do not cross. Press the button on the box and wait. When the lights change to show a steady green figure check that the traffic has stopped and then cross with care. (At some Pelicans there is also a bleeping sound or voice to tell blind or partially sighted people when the steady green figure is showing.) After a while, the green figure will begin to flash. This means that you should not start to cross. But if you have already started you will have time to finish crossing safely.

15. A 'staggered' crossing (see illustration) should be treated as two separate crossings. On reaching the central island you must press the button again to obtain a steady green figure.

Treat staggered crossings as two separate crossings.

At traffic lights and Pelican crossings

At Pelicans only

Do not cross

Cross with care

Do not start to cross

Crossing at a Puffin crossing

16. Puffin crossings are similar to Pelican crossings except that the pedestrian signals are on your side of the road. After pressing the button, you should wait where indicated for the green figure to show. Detectors will vary the length of time of the red light for drivers to ensure that pedestrians have enough time to cross safely.

Crossing at traffic lights

17. Some traffic lights have pedestrian signals similar to those at Pelican crossings. The green figure does not flash but there will be enough time to finish crossing after it goes out. If there are no pedestrian signals, watch carefully and do not cross until the traffic lights are red and the traffic has stopped. Even then, look out for traffic turning the corner. Remember that traffic lights may let traffic move in some lanes while other lanes are stopped.

Crossings controlled by police, traffic wardens or school crossing patrols

18. Where a police officer, traffic warden or school crossing patrol is controlling the traffic, do not cross the road until they signal you to do so. Always cross in front of them.

Guard rails

19. Guard rails are there for your safety. Cross the road only at the gaps provided for pedestrians. Do not climb over the guard rails or walk between them and the road.

Tactile paving

20. Some pedestrian crossing points have textured paving to let blind or partially sighted people know where to stand while waiting to cross the road.

Crossing one-way streets

21. Use the Green Cross Code. Check which way the traffic is moving. Do not cross until it is safe to do so without stopping. In some one-way streets, bus lanes operate in the opposite direction to the rest of the traffic.

Crossing bus and cycle lanes

22. Use the Green Cross Code. Vehicles in bus lanes may be going faster than traffic in other lanes. Watch out for cyclists who may be riding in bus or cycle lanes.

Parked vehicles

23. If you have to cross between parked vehicles, use the outside edge of the vehicles as if it were the kerb. Stop there and make sure you can see all around and that the traffic can see you. Then carry on using the Green Cross Code. Do not stand in front of or behind any vehicle that has its engine running.

Crossing the road at night

24. Use the Green Cross Code. If there is no pedestrian crossing or central island nearby, cross near a street light so that traffic can see you more easily. It is harder for others to see you at night so wear something reflective.

EMERGENCY VEHICLES

25. If you see or hear ambulances, fire engines, police or other emergency vehicles with their blue lights flashing or their sirens sounding, **KEEP OFF THE ROAD**.

GETTING ON OR OFF A BUS

26. Only get on or off a bus when it has stopped to allow you to do so. Never cross the road directly behind or in front of a bus. Wait until it has moved off and you can see the road clearly in both directions.

RAILWAYS AND TRAMWAYS

27. Take extra care at railway level crossings and near tramways (see Rules 225–234 and 241–242).

DRIVERS, MOTORCYCLISTS AND CYCLISTS

(More detailed guidance is given in The Driving Standards Agency's publications *The Driving Manual* and *The Motorcycling Manual*.)

GENERAL

Vehicle condition

28. You **MUST** ensure your vehicle is roadworthy. Take special care of lights, brakes, steering, tyres (including spare), exhaust system, seat belts, demisters, windscreen wipers and washers. Keep windscreens, windows, lights, indicators, reflectors, mirrors and number plates clean and clear. Ensure your seat, seat belt, head restraint and mirrors are adjusted correctly before you drive.

Loads

29. Any loads carried or towed **MUST** be secure and **MUST NOT** stick out dangerously. You **MUST NOT** overload your vehicle or trailer.

Motorcycles

30. The rider and pillion passenger on a motorcycle, scooter or moped **MUST** wear an approved safety helmet which **MUST** be fastened securely. It is also advisable to wear eye protectors, and strong boots, gloves and clothes that will help protect you if you fall off. Pillion passengers **MUST** sit astride the machine on a proper seat and keep both feet on the footrests. To help you to be seen, wear something light-coloured or bright. Fluorescent material helps in the daylight, as do dipped headlights on larger machines. Reflective material helps in the dark.

Tiredness or illness

31. If you feel tired or ill, **DO NOT DRIVE**.

32. Driving can make you feel sleepy. To help avoid this, make sure there is a supply of fresh air into your vehicle. If you feel tired while driving, find a safe place to stop and rest.

33. You **MUST NOT** drive under the influence of drugs or medicines. When taking prescribed medicines, ask your doctor if it is safe to drive. When taking other medicines, ask the pharmacist.

Vision
34. You **MUST** be able to read a vehicle number plate from a distance of 20.5 metres (67 ft) which is about five car lengths. If you need glasses (or contact lenses) to do this you **MUST** wear them when driving.

35. At night or in poor visibility, do not use tinted glasses, lenses or visors. Do not use spray-on or other tinting materials for windows and windscreens.

Learners
36. Learner drivers in a car **MUST** be supervised by someone at least 21 years old who has held a full British licence for that type of car (automatic or manual) for at least three years and still holds one.

37. If you are learning to ride a motorcycle, scooter or moped you **MUST** take basic training with an approved training body before riding on the road, unless exempt. You **MUST NOT** carry a pillion passenger, pull a trailer or ride a solo motorcycle with an engine capacity in excess of 125cc.

38. All vehicles under the control of a learner **MUST** display L-plates. In Wales, either D-plates, L-plates, or both, can be used. Plates should be removed or covered at all other times (except on driving school vehicles).

Alcohol and the motorist
39. Do not drink and drive. Drinking alcohol seriously affects your driving. It reduces your co-ordination, slows down your reactions, affects your judgement of speed, distance and risk, and gives you a false sense of confidence. Your driving may be badly affected even if you are below the legal limit (see page 68).

Remember: you may still be unfit to drive in the evening after drinking at lunchtime or in the morning after drinking the previous evening.

Seat belts

40. Wearing seat belts saves lives and reduces the risk of serious injury in an accident. You **MUST** wear a seat belt if one is available, unless you are exempt.

The following table summarises the main legal requirements for wearing seat belts.

	FRONT SEAT	REAR SEAT	WHOSE RESPONSIBILITY
DRIVER	Must be worn if fitted	—	Driver
CHILD UNDER 3 YEARS OF AGE	Appropriate child restraint must be worn	Appropriate child restraint must be worn if available	Driver
CHILD AGED 3 to 11 and under 1.5 metres (about 5 feet) in height	Appropriate child restraint must be worn if available. If not, an adult seat belt must be worn	Appropriate child restraint must be worn if available. If not, an adult seat belt must be worn if available	Driver
CHILD AGED 12 or 13 or younger child 1.5 metres or more in height	Adult seat belt must be worn if available	Adult seat belt must be worn if available	Driver
ADULT PASSENGERS	Must be worn if available	Must be worn if available	Passenger

41. An appropriate child restraint is a baby carrier, child seat, harness or booster seat appropriate to the child's weight.

Children in cars

42. Do not let children sit behind the rear seats in an estate car or hatchback. Make sure that child safety door locks, where fitted, are used when children are in the car. Keep children under control in the car.

Car telephones and microphones
43. You **MUST** exercise proper control of your vehicle at all times. Do not use a hand-held telephone or microphone while you are driving. Find a safe place to stop first. Do not speak into a hands-free microphone if it will take your mind off the road. You **MUST NOT** stop on the hard shoulder of a motorway to answer or make a call, except in an emergency.

Traffic light signals and traffic signs
44. You **MUST** obey all traffic light signals (see page 54) and traffic signs giving orders (see pages 58 and 59). Make sure you also know and act on all other traffic signs and road markings (see pages 59 to 65).

Signals
45. Give signals to help and warn other road users, including pedestrians (see pages 56 and 57). Give them clearly and in plenty of time. Make sure your indicators are cancelled after use.

46. Watch out for signals given by other road users and take appropriate action.

47. You **MUST** obey signals by police officers and traffic wardens (see page 55) and signs used by school crossing patrols.

DRIVING YOUR VEHICLE

Moving off
48. Use your mirrors before you move off. Signal if necessary before moving out. Look round as well for a final check. Only move off when it is safe to do so.

Driving along
49. Keep to the left, except where road signs or markings indicate otherwise or when you want to overtake, turn right or pass parked vehicles or pedestrians in the road. Let others overtake you if they want to.

50. You **MUST NOT** drive on a pavement or footpath except for access to property.

51. Use your mirrors frequently so you always know what is behind and to each side of you. Use them well before you carry out a manoeuvre or change speed; then give the correct signal if you need to. Motorcyclists should always look behind before manoeuvring.

Remember: mirrors–signal–manoeuvre

52. Watch out for cycles and motorcycles. Two-wheelers are far harder to spot than larger vehicles – but their riders have the same rights as other road users and are particularly vulnerable. Give riders plenty of room, especially if you are driving a long vehicle or towing a trailer.

53. Do not hold up a long queue of traffic. If you are driving a large or slow-moving vehicle and the road is narrow or winding, or there is a lot of traffic coming towards you, pull in where you can do so safely so that other vehicles can overtake.

Speed limits
54. You **MUST NOT** exceed the maximum speed limits for the road and for your vehicle (see the table on page 53). Street lights usually indicate a 30 mph speed limit unless signs show other limits.

55. Drive slowly in residential areas. In some roads there are features such as road humps and narrowings intended to slow you down. A 20 mph maximum speed limit may also be in force.

56. A speed limit does not mean it is safe to drive at that speed. Drive according to the conditions. Slow down if the road is wet or icy and in fog. Drive more slowly at night when it is harder to see pedestrians and cyclists.

Stopping distances
57. Drive at a speed that will allow you to stop well within the distance you can see to be clear. Leave enough space between you and the vehicle in front so that you can pull up safely if it suddenly slows down or stops. The safe rule is never to get closer than the overall stopping distances shown opposite. But in good conditions on roads carrying fast traffic, a two second time gap may be sufficient. The gap should be at least doubled on wet roads and increased further on icy roads. Large

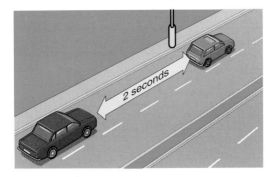

Use stationary objects (eg lamp-posts) to help you keep a two second gap.

2 seconds

vehicles and motorcycles need more time to stop than cars. Drop back if someone overtakes and pulls into the gap in front of you.

	Shortest stopping distances – in metres and feet			
mph	Thinking distance	Braking distance	Overall stopping distance	On a dry road, a good car with good brakes and tyres and an alert driver will stop in the distances shown. Remember these are shortest stopping distances. Stopping distances increase greatly with wet and slippery roads, poor brakes and tyres, and tired drivers.
20	6 20	6 20	12 40	
30	9 30	14 45	23 75	
40	12 40	24 80	36 120	
50	15 50	38 125	53 175	
60	18 60	55 180	73 240	
70	21 70	75 245	96 315	
(See diagram on back cover)				

Fog code

58. Before driving in fog, consider if your journey is essential. If it is, allow extra time. Make sure your windscreen, windows and lights are clean and that all your lights (including brake lights) are working.

When driving in fog:

● See and be seen. If you cannot see clearly use dipped headlights. Use front or rear fog lights if visibility is seriously reduced (see Rule 133) but switch them off when visibility improves. Use your windscreen wipers and demisters.

● Check your mirrors and slow down. Keep a safe distance behind the vehicle in front. You should always be able to pull up within the distance you can see clearly.

- Do not hang on to the tail lights of the vehicle in front; it gives a false sense of security. In thick fog, if you can see the vehicle in front you are probably too close unless you are travelling very slowly.
- Be aware of your speed; you may be going much faster than you think. Do not accelerate to get away from a vehicle which is too close behind you. When you slow down, use your brakes so that your brake lights warn drivers behind you.
- When the word 'Fog' is shown on a roadside signal but the road appears to be clear, be prepared for a bank of fog or drifting smoke ahead. Fog can drift rapidly and is often patchy. Even if it seems to be clearing, you can suddenly find yourself back in thick fog.

Winter driving

59. Prepare your vehicle for winter. Ensure that the battery is well maintained and that there are appropriate anti-freeze agents in the radiator and windscreen washer bottle.

60. In freezing or near freezing conditions, drive with great care even if the roads have been gritted. Roads may be slippery and surface conditions can change abruptly. Take care when overtaking gritting vehicles, particularly if you are riding a motorcycle.

61. Do not drive in snow unless your journey is essential. If it is, drive slowly but keep in as high a gear as possible to help avoid wheel spin. Avoid harsh acceleration, steering and braking. You **MUST** use headlights when visibility is seriously reduced by falling snow (see Rule 131).

62. Watch out for snow-ploughs which may throw out snow on either side. Do not overtake them unless the lane you intend to use has been cleared of snow.

The safety of pedestrians

63. Show consideration to pedestrians. Drive carefully and slowly when there are pedestrians about, especially in crowded shopping streets or residential areas and near bus and tram stops, parked milk floats or mobile shops. Watch out for pedestrians emerging suddenly into the road, especially from behind parked vehicles.

64.   Watch out for children and elderly pedestrians who may not be able to judge your speed and could step into the road in front of you. Watch out for blind and partially sighted people who may be carrying white sticks (white with two red reflective bands for deaf and blind people) or using guide dogs and for people with other disabilities. Give them plenty of time to cross the road. Do not assume that a pedestrian can hear your vehicle coming; they may have hearing difficulties.

65.   Drive slowly near schools. In some places, there may be a flashing amber signal below the 'School' warning sign which tells you that there may be children crossing the road ahead. When these signals are flashing, drive very slowly until you are well clear of the area. Drive carefully when passing a stationary bus showing a 'School Bus' sign (see page 66) as children may be getting on or off.

66.   You **MUST** stop when a school crossing patrol shows a 'STOP' for children sign (see page 58).

67.   Be careful near a parked ice-cream van – children are more interested in ice-cream than in traffic.

Watch out for children.

68. At road junctions, give way to pedestrians who are already crossing the road into which you are turning.

69. Give way to pedestrians on a pavement you need to cross, eg to reach a driveway.

Remember: pavements are for people – not for vehicles

70. Be prepared for pedestrians walking in the road, especially on narrow country roads. Give them plenty of room. Take extra care on left-hand bends and keep your speed down.

Pedestrian crossings
71. As you approach a Zebra crossing, look out for people waiting to cross (especially children, elderly people or people with disabilities). Be ready to slow down or stop to let them cross. When someone has stepped on to a crossing, you **MUST** give way. Allow more time for stopping on wet or icy roads. Do not wave people across; this could be dangerous if another vehicle is approaching.

72. You **MUST NOT** overtake or park on a Zebra, Puffin or Pelican crossing, including the area marked by zigzag lines. Even when there are no zigzags, do not overtake just before the crossing.

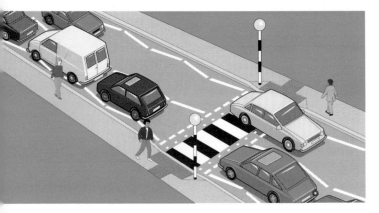

Keep pedestrian crossings clear.

73. In a queue of traffic, you **MUST** keep pedestrian crossings clear.

74. At Pelican crossings a flashing amber light will follow the red 'STOP' light. When the amber light is flashing, you **MUST** give way to any pedestrians on the crossing. A Pelican crossing which goes straight across the road is one crossing even when there is a central island and you **MUST** wait for pedestrians crossing from the other side of the island. Do not harass pedestrians – for example, by revving your engine.

Give way to pedestrians.

75. At pedestrian crossings controlled by lights, give way to pedestrians who are still crossing after the signal for vehicles has changed to green.

Emergency vehicles

76. Look and listen for ambulances, fire engines, police or other emergency vehicles with flashing blue lights or sirens. Make room for them to pass (if necessary by pulling to the side of the road and stopping) but do not endanger other road users. A flashing green light on a vehicle indicates a doctor answering an emergency call so give way as soon as possible.

Flashing amber lights on vehicles

77. Drive carefully when you see a flashing amber light as it warns of a slow-moving vehicle (such as a road gritter or tractor) or a vehicle which has broken down.

Police stopping procedures

78. If the police want to stop your vehicle they will, where possible, attract your attention from behind by flashing their headlights or blue light or by sounding their siren or horn. A police officer will direct you to pull over to the side by pointing and using the left indicator. You **MUST** pull over and stop as soon as it is safe to do so and then switch off your engine.

Buses
79. Give way to buses whenever you can do so safely, especially when they signal to pull away from bus stops. Look out for people leaving the bus and crossing the road.

Animals
80. Watch out for animals being led or ridden on the road and take extra care at left-hand bends and on narrow country roads. Drive slowly past animals. Give them plenty of room and be ready to stop. Do not scare animals by sounding your horn or revving your engine.

81. Look out for horse riders' signals and be aware that they may not move to the centre of the road prior to turning right. Riders of horses and ponies are often children – so take extra care.

Single-track roads
82. Some roads (often called single-track roads) are only wide enough for one vehicle. They may have special passing places. Pull into a passing place on your left, or wait opposite a passing place on your right, when you see a vehicle coming towards you, or the driver behind you wants to overtake. Give way to vehicles coming uphill whenever you can. Do not park in passing places.

LINES AND LANES ALONG THE ROAD

83. A single broken line, with long markings and short gaps, along the centre of the road is a hazard warning line (see page 65). Do not cross it unless you can see that the road is clear well ahead.

84. Where there are double white lines along the road and the line nearest you is unbroken, you **MUST NOT** cross or straddle it unless it is safe to do so and you need to do so to enter adjoining premises, or a side road, to pass a stationary vehicle, or pass a road maintenance vehicle, pedal cycle or horse moving at 10 mph or less.

85. Where there are double white lines along the road and the line nearest to you is broken, you may cross the lines to overtake if it is safe, provided you can do so before reaching an unbroken white line on your side.

86. Areas of white diagonal stripes or white chevrons painted on the road are to separate traffic lanes or to protect traffic turning right. Where the marked area is bordered by an unbroken white line, you **MUST NOT** enter it except in an emergency. Where the line is broken, you should not enter the area unless you can see that it is safe to do so.

87. Short broken white lines divide the road into lanes – keep between them. Coloured reflecting road studs may be used with white lines – white studs to mark the lanes or middle of the road, red studs to mark the left edge of the road and amber studs by the central reservation of a dual carriageway. Green studs may be used across lay-bys and side roads.

88. On some hills an extra uphill 'crawler' lane may be provided. Use this lane if you are driving a slow-moving vehicle or if there are vehicles behind you wishing to overtake.

Lane discipline
89. If you need to change lane, first use your mirrors to make sure you will not force another driver or rider to swerve or slow down. If it is safe to move over, signal before you do so.

Remember: mirrors–signal–manoeuvre

90. At some junctions, lanes may go in different directions. Follow the signs and get into the correct lane in good time.

91. In a traffic hold-up, do not try to 'jump the queue' by cutting into another lane or by overtaking the vehicles in front of you.

92. Where a single carriageway has three lanes and the road markings do not give priority to traffic in either direction, use the middle lane only for overtaking or turning right. Remember – you have no more right to use the middle lane than a driver coming from the opposite direction. Do not use the right-hand lane.

93. Where a single carriageway has four or more lanes, do not use the lanes on the right-hand side of the road unless signs and markings indicate that you can.

94. On a two-lane dual carriageway, use the right-hand lane only for overtaking or turning right.

95. On a three-lane dual carriageway, stay in the left-hand lane. If there are slower vehicles than you in that lane, use the middle lane to overtake them but return to the left-hand lane when it is clear. The right-hand lane is for overtaking (or turning right); if you use it for overtaking, move back into the middle lane and then into the left-hand lane as soon as it is safe to do so.

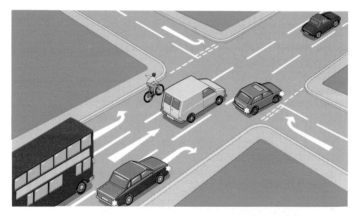

Choose the correct lane.

96. In one-way streets, choose the correct lane for your exit as soon as you can. Do not change lanes suddenly. Unless road signs or markings indicate otherwise, choose the left-hand lane when going to the left, the right-hand lane when going to the right and the most appropriate lane when going straight ahead. Remember – traffic could be passing on both sides.

97. Bus and tram lanes are shown by road markings and signs. You **MUST NOT** drive in a tram lane or in a bus lane during its period of operation unless the signs indicate you may do so.

98. Cycle lanes are shown by road markings and signs. You **MUST NOT** drive or park in a cycle lane marked by an unbroken white line during its period of operation. Do not drive in a cycle lane marked by a broken white line unless it is unavoidable.

OVERTAKING

99. Do not overtake unless you can do so safely. Make sure the road is sufficiently clear ahead and behind. Do not get too close to the vehicle you intend to overtake – it will obscure your view of the road ahead. Use your mirrors. Signal before you start to move out. Take extra care at night and in poor visibility when it is harder to judge speed and distance.

Remember: mirrors–signal–manoeuvre

100. Once you have started to overtake, quickly move past the vehicle you are overtaking, leaving it plenty of room. Then move back to the left as soon as you can but do not cut in.

Give riders plenty of room when overtaking.

101. When overtaking motorcyclists, pedal-cyclists or horse riders, give them at least as much room as you would give a car. Remember that cyclists may be unable to ride in a straight line, especially when it is windy or the road surface is uneven.

102. Do not overtake on the left unless:

- the vehicle in front is signalling to turn right, and you can overtake on the left safely;
- traffic is moving slowly in queues and vehicles in a lane on the right are moving more slowly than you are.

103. In slow-moving traffic queues, move to a lane on your left only to turn left. Do not change lanes to the left to overtake. Cyclists and motorcyclists overtaking traffic queues should watch out for pedestrians crossing between vehicles and vehicles emerging from junctions.

104. Do not increase your speed when you are being overtaken. Slow down if necessary to let the overtaking vehicle pass and pull in.

105. On a two-lane single carriageway give way to vehicles coming towards you before passing parked vehicles or other obstructions on your side of the road.

106. **a** You **MUST NOT** overtake:

- if you would have to cross or straddle double white lines with an unbroken line nearest to you (see Rule 84);
- if you are in the zigzag area at a pedestrian crossing;
- after a 'No Overtaking' sign and until you pass a sign cancelling the restriction;

b **DO NOT** overtake:

i) where you cannot see far enough ahead to be sure it is safe, for example when you are approaching or at:
- a corner or bend;
- a hump bridge;
- the brow of a hill; or

ii) where you might come into conflict with other road users, for example:

- approaching or at a road junction on either side of the road;
- where the road narrows;
- when approaching a school crossing patrol;
- where you would have to drive over an area marked with diagonal stripes or chevrons;
- where you would have to enter a lane reserved for buses, trams or cyclists;
- between a bus or tram and the kerb when it is at a stop;
- where traffic is queuing at junctions or road works;
- when you would force another vehicle to swerve or slow down;
- at a level crossing.

If in doubt – do not overtake

ROAD JUNCTIONS

107. Take extra care at junctions. Check your position and speed. Junctions are particularly dangerous for cyclists, motorcyclists and pedestrians, so watch out for them before you turn. Watch out for long vehicles which may be turning at a junction ahead; they may have to use the whole width of the road to make the turn.

Give way to pedestrians.

108. Give way to pedestrians crossing a road into which you are turning.

109. At a junction with a 'STOP' sign and an unbroken white line across the road, you **MUST**

stop behind the line. Wait for a safe gap in the traffic before you move off.

110. At a junction with broken white lines across the road (it may also have a 'Give Way' sign or a triangle marked on the road), you **MUST** give way to traffic on the other road.

111. When waiting at a junction, do not assume that a vehicle coming from the right and signalling left will do so. Wait and make sure.

112. When going straight across or turning right into a dual carriageway, treat each half as a separate road. Wait in the central reservation until there is a safe gap in the traffic on the second half of the road. If the central reservation is too narrow for the length of your vehicle, wait until you can cross both carriageways in one go.

113. Box junctions have criss-cross yellow lines painted on the road (see page 65). You **MUST NOT** enter the box until your exit road or lane from it is clear. But you may enter the box when you want to turn right and are only stopped from doing so by oncoming traffic or by vehicles waiting to turn right.

Do not go forward unless you can clear the junction.

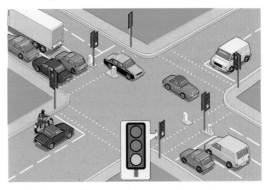

Junctions controlled by traffic lights

114. At junctions controlled by traffic lights, you **MUST** stop behind the white 'STOP' line across your side of the road unless the light is green. You **MUST NOT** move forward when the red and amber lights are showing. Do not go forward when the traffic lights are green unless there is room for you to

clear the junction safely or you are taking up a
position to turn right.

**Get into the
correct lane.**

115. Where traffic lights have a green filter
arrow indicating a filter-only lane, do not enter that
lane unless you want to go in the direction of the
arrow. Give other traffic, especially cyclists, room
to move into the correct lane.

116. If the traffic lights are not working,
proceed with caution.

Turning right

117. Well before you turn right, use your
mirrors to make sure you know the position and
movement of traffic behind you. Give a right-turn
signal and, as soon as it is safe for you to do so,
take up a position just left of the middle of the
road or in the space marked for right-turning
traffic. If possible leave room for other vehicles to
pass on the left. Wait until there is a safe gap
between you and any oncoming vehicle. Watch out
for cyclists, motorcyclists and pedestrians; then
make the turn, but do not cut the corner. Take
great care when turning into a main road; you will
need to watch for traffic in both directions and
wait for a safe gap.

Remember: mirrors–signal–manoeuvre

Turn offside-to-offside if possible.

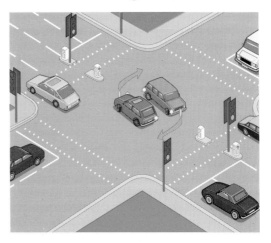

118. When turning right at a junction where an oncoming vehicle is also turning right, it is normally safer to keep the other vehicle to your right and turn behind it: ie offside-to-offside. Before you complete the turn, check for other traffic on the road you want to cross.

Take care when turning nearside-to-nearside.

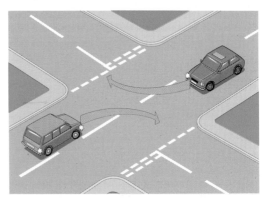

119. If the lay-out of the junction or the traffic situation makes offside-to-offside passing impracticable, pass nearside-to-nearside, but take care. The other vehicle could obstruct your view of the road so watch carefully for oncoming traffic.

120. When turning right from a dual carriageway, wait in the opening in the central reservation until you are sure it is safe to cross the other carriageway.

Turning left

121.   Well before you turn left, use your mirrors and give a left-turn signal. Do not overtake a cyclist, motorcyclist or horse rider immediately before turning left and watch out for traffic coming up on your left before you make the turn. When turning, keep as close to the left as it is safe to do so.

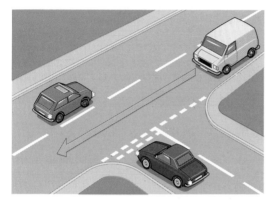

Wait for a safe gap before turning.

122.   If you want to turn left across a bus lane, cycle lane or tramway, give way to any vehicles using it from either direction.

ROUNDABOUTS

123.   On approaching a roundabout, decide as early as possible which exit you need to take and get into the correct lane. Reduce your speed. On reaching the roundabout, give way to traffic on your right unless road markings indicate otherwise. Watch out for traffic already on the roundabout, especially cyclists and motorcyclists. At some junctions there may be more than one roundabout. At each one, use the normal rules for roundabouts.

124.   Unless signs or road markings indicate otherwise:

● When turning left:
  – signal left and approach in the left-hand lane;

– keep to the left on the roundabout and
   continue signalling left.
● When going straight ahead:
 – do not signal on approach;
 – approach in the left-hand or centre lane on a
   three-lane road (on a two-lane road you may
   approach in the right-hand lane if the left-hand
   lane is blocked);
 – take the same course on the roundabout;
 – signal left after you have passed the exit
   before the one you want.
● When turning right or going full circle:
 – signal right and approach in the right-hand lane;
 – keep to the right on the roundabout;
 – continue to signal right until you have passed
   the exit before the one you want, then signal left.

When there are more than three lanes at the
entrance to a roundabout, use the most appropriate
lane on approach and through the roundabout.

125.   Watch out for traffic crossing in front of
you on the roundabout, especially vehicles intending
to leave by the next exit. Show them consideration.

126.   Watch out for motorcyclists, cyclists and
horse riders. Give them plenty of room. Cyclists
and horse riders will often keep to the left on the
roundabout; they may also indicate right to show
they are continuing around the roundabout.

127.   Long vehicles may have to take a different

**Follow the
correct
procedure at
roundabouts.**

course, both approaching and on the roundabout.
Watch for their signals and give them plenty of room.

128. The same rules apply to mini-roundabouts.
If possible, pass around the central marking. Watch
out for vehicles making a U-turn and for long
vehicles which may have to cross the centre of the
mini-roundabout.

**Follow the
correct
procedure at
roundabouts.**

REVERSING

129. Before reversing make sure there are no
pedestrians – particularly children – or obstructions
in the road behind you. Be aware of the 'blind spot'
behind you – the part of the road you cannot see
from the driving seat. Reverse with care. If you
cannot see clearly, get someone to guide you. You
MUST NOT reverse your vehicle for longer than
necessary.

**Reverse with
care.**

130. **NEVER** reverse from a side-road into a main road. Avoid reversing into the road from a driveway; where possible, reverse in and drive out.

VEHICLE LIGHTS

131. You **MUST**:

● make sure all your lights are clean, that they work and that your headlights are properly adjusted – badly adjusted headlights can dazzle other road users and may cause accidents;
● use sidelights between sunset and sunrise;
● use headlights at night (between half an hour after sunset and half an hour before sunrise) on all roads without street lighting and on roads where the street lights are more than 185 metres (600 ft) apart or are not lit;
● use headlights or front fog lights when visibility is seriously reduced, generally when you cannot see for more than 100 metres (328 ft).

132. You should also:

● use headlights at night on lit motorways and roads with a speed limit in excess of 50 mph;
● use dipped headlights at night in built-up areas unless the road is well lit;
● cut down glare. If your vehicle has dim-dip, use it instead of dipped headlights in dull daytime weather and at night in built-up areas with good street lighting;
● dip your headlights when meeting vehicles or other road users and before you dazzle the driver of a vehicle you are following;
● slow down or stop if you are dazzled by oncoming headlights.

Fog lights
133. Use fog lights when visibility is seriously reduced, generally when you cannot see for more than 100 metres (328 ft). You **MUST NOT** use fog lights at other times. Remember to switch them off when visibility improves.

Hazard warning lights

134. Hazard warning lights may be used when your vehicle is stopped to warn that it is temporarily obstructing traffic. You may only use them whilst driving if you are on a motorway or unrestricted dual carriageway and you need to warn drivers behind you of a hazard or obstruction ahead. Only use them for just long enough to ensure that your warning has been observed. Never use them as an excuse for dangerous or illegal parking.

Flashing headlights

135. Flashing your headlights means only one thing – it lets another road user know you are there. Do not flash your headlights for any other reason and never assume that it is a signal to proceed.

Use of the horn

136. When your vehicle is moving, use your horn only if you need to warn other road users of your presence. Never sound your horn aggressively. You **MUST NOT** use your horn;

- between 11.30 pm and 7.00 am in a built-up area;
- when your vehicle is stationary, unless a moving vehicle poses a danger.

WAITING AND PARKING

137. Wherever possible, pull off the road on to an area provided for parking. If you have to stop on the road, stop as close as you can to the side. Leave plenty of room when parking next to or behind a vehicle displaying a disabled person's badge. Before you or your passengers open a door, make sure it will not hit anyone passing on the road or pavement or force them to swerve; watch out particularly for pedestrians, cyclists and motorcyclists. It is safer for you and your passengers (especially children) to get out on the side next to the kerb. You **MUST** switch off the engine and headlights. Before leaving the vehicle, ensure that the handbrake is on firmly. Always lock your vehicle.

138. You **MUST NOT** stop or park on:

- the carriageway of a motorway (see Rules 179–180);
- a pedestrian crossing, including the area marked by the zig-zag lines (see Rule 72);
- a Clearway (see page 58);
- an Urban Clearway within its hours of operation except to pick up or set down passengers (see page 58);
- a road marked with double white lines even if one of the lines is broken, except to pick up or set down passengers;
- a bus, tram or cycle lane during its period of operation.

139. You **MUST NOT** park where there are parking restrictions shown by yellow lines along the edge of the carriageway (see page 64), or red lines in the case of specially designated 'red routes'. The periods when restrictions apply are indicated by signs either adjacent to the kerb or on entry to a controlled parking zone. Use an authorised parking space if one is available.

140. Think before you park. **DO NOT** park your vehicle where it would endanger or inconvenience pedestrians or other road users, for example:

- on a footpath, pavement or cycle track;
- near a school entrance;
- at or near a bus stop or taxi rank;
- on the approach to a level crossing;
- within 10 metres (32 ft) of a junction, except in an authorised parking space;
- near the brow of a hill or hump bridge;
- opposite a traffic island or (if this would cause an obstruction) another parked vehicle;
- where you would force other traffic to enter a tram lane;
- where the kerb has been lowered to help wheelchair users;
- in front of the entrance to a property.

141. You **MUST NOT** park in a parking space reserved for specific users, such as Orange Badge holders or residents, unless entitled to do so.

Parking at night
142. You **MUST NOT** park at night facing against the direction of the traffic flow.

143. When parking on the road at night, you **MUST** leave your sidelights on. However cars, goods vehicles not exceeding 1525 kg unladen, invalid carriages and motorcycles may be parked without lights on a road with a speed limit of 30 mph or less if they are:

● at least 10 metres (32 ft) away from any junction, close to the kerb and facing in the direction of the traffic flow; or
● in a recognised parking place.

Other vehicles and trailers, and all vehicles with projecting loads, **MUST NOT** be left on a road at night without lights.

Parking in fog
144. It is especially dangerous to park on the road in fog. If it is unavoidable, leave your sidelights on.

Loading and unloading
145. Restrictions on loading and unloading are shown by yellow markings on the kerb (see page 64). Loading and unloading may be permitted when parking is otherwise restricted.

146. Goods vehicles with a maximum laden weight of over 7.5 tonnes (including any trailer) **MUST NOT** be parked on a central reservation without police permission or on a verge or footway, except where this is essential for loading or unloading (in which case the vehicle **MUST NOT** be left unattended).

ROAD WORKS

147. Special care is needed at road works. Watch out for and act on all signs on the approach to and at road works (see page 63). Use your mirrors and get into the correct lane for your vehicle in good time. Do not switch lanes to overtake queuing traffic or drive through an area marked off by traffic cones. Watch out for traffic entering or leaving the works area, but do not be distracted by what is going on there.

148. You **MUST NOT** exceed any temporary maximum speed limit.

BREAKDOWNS AND ACCIDENTS

149. If you have a breakdown, think first of other traffic. Get your vehicle off the road if possible.

150. If your vehicle is causing an obstruction, warn other traffic by using your hazard warning lights. If you carry a red warning triangle, put it on the road at least 50 metres (164 ft) before the obstruction and on the same side of the road (150 metres [492 ft] on the hard shoulder of motorways). At night or in poor visibility, do not stand behind your vehicle or let anyone else do so – you could prevent other drivers seeing your rear lights.

151. If anything falls from your vehicle on to the road, stop and retrieve it as soon as it is safe to do so (for motorways see Rule 178).

152. If you see warning signs or the flashing lights of emergency vehicles or vehicles in the distance moving very slowly or stopped, there could have been an accident. Slow down and be ready to stop. Do not be distracted when passing the accident; you could cause another one.

153. If you are involved in, or stop to give assistance at, an accident:

- warn other traffic, eg by switching on your hazard warning lights. Ask drivers to switch off their engines and put out any cigarettes;
- arrange for the emergency services to be called immediately with full details of the accident location and any casualties; on a motorway, use the emergency telephone;
- do not move injured people from their vehicles unless they are in immediate danger from fire or explosion. Do not remove a motorcyclist's

helmet unless it is essential. Be prepared to give first aid as shown on pages 75 and 76;

● move uninjured people away from the vehicles to safety; on a motorway this should be well away from the traffic, the hard shoulder and the central reservation;

● stay at the scene until emergency services arrive.

Accidents involving dangerous goods

154. Vehicles carrying dangerous goods in packages will be marked with plain orange reflectorised plates. Road tankers and vehicles carrying tank containers will have hazard warning plates (see page 66). If an accident involves a vehicle containing dangerous goods, follow the advice in Rule 153 and, in particular:

● switch off engines and **DO NOT SMOKE**;

● keep uninjured people well away from the vehicle and where the wind will not blow dangerous substances towards them. Even if you act to save a life, take care that you too are not affected by dangerous substances;

● give the emergency services as much information as possible about the labels and other markings.

MOTORWAYS

Many other Rules also apply to motorway driving, either wholly or in part: Rules 28–35, 39–49, 51, 52, 54, 56–62, 76–78, 87, 89–91, 94, 95, 131–136, 138, 147–150, 152–154 and 213.

GENERAL

155. Motorways **MUST NOT** be used by pedestrians, provisional licence holders, riders of motorcycles under 50cc, cyclists and horse riders. Slow-moving vehicles, agricultural vehicles and some invalid carriages are also prohibited. (See page 71.)

156. Traffic on motorways travels more quickly than on other roads, so you have to think quickly too. It is especially important to use your mirrors earlier and look much further ahead than you would on other roads.

157. Make sure your vehicle is fit to cruise at speed, has correct tyre pressures and enough fuel, oil and water to get you at least to the next service area. See that the windscreen, windows, mirrors, lights and reflectors are clean and that the windscreen washer bottle is topped up. You **MUST** make sure that any load you are carrying or towing is secure.

JOINING THE MOTORWAY

158. When you join the motorway you will normally approach it from a road on the left (a slip-road). You **MUST** give way to traffic already on the motorway. While on the slip-road, check the traffic already on the motorway and adjust your speed so that you join the left-hand lane where there is a safe gap and at the same speed as traffic in that lane.

159. At some junctions the slip-road will continue as an extra lane on the motorway. Where signs indicate that this will happen, stay in that lane until it becomes part of the motorway.

160. After joining the motorway, stay in the left-hand lane long enough to get used to the speed of traffic before overtaking.

ON THE MOTORWAY

161. When you can see well ahead and the road conditions are good, drive at a steady cruising speed which you and your vehicle can handle easily. You **MUST NOT** exceed the maximum speed limit for your vehicle (see page 53). Keep a safe distance from the vehicle in front and increase the gap on wet or icy roads, or in fog (see Rules 57–58).

162. Driving can make you feel sleepy. To help prevent this, make sure there is a supply of fresh air into your vehicle, stop at a service area or leave the motorway and find a safe place to stop.

163. You **MUST NOT** reverse, cross the central reservation, or drive against the traffic flow. Even if you have missed your exit, or have taken the wrong route, carry on to the next exit.

Lane discipline
164. Keep in the left-hand lane unless overtaking. You may use the lane to the right of a stream of slower vehicles to overtake them but return to the lane to your left when you have passed them.

165. When approaching a junction make sure you are in the correct lane; at some junctions a lane may lead directly off the motorway.

166. Some vehicles **MUST NOT** use the right-hand lane of a motorway with three or more lanes (see page 71).

Overtaking
167. Overtake only on the right unless traffic is moving in queues and the queue on your right is moving more slowly than you are. Do not move to a lane on your left to overtake. You **MUST NOT** use the hard shoulder for overtaking.

Do not get too close to the vehicle you are going to overtake.

168. Do not overtake unless you are sure it is safe to do so. Before you start to overtake, make sure that the lane you will be joining is sufficiently clear ahead and behind. Use your mirrors.

Remember that traffic may be coming up behind you very quickly. Signal before you move out. Be especially careful at night and in poor visibility when it is harder to judge speed and distance.

169. Always get back to the left-hand lane or, if it is occupied, the middle lane, as soon as you can after overtaking. Signal your intention to change lanes. Do not cut in on the vehicle you have overtaken.

Remember: mirrors–signal–manoeuvre

Motorway signals
170. Motorway signals (see page 54) are used to warn you of a danger ahead, for example an accident or risk of skidding. Usually they are situated on the central reservation where they apply to all lanes. On very busy stretches, they may be overhead with a signal for each lane.

171. Where there is danger, amber lights flash. The signal may also show a temporary maximum speed limit, lanes that are closed or a message (for example, 'Fog'). Reduce your speed and look out for the danger until you pass a signal which is not flashing and you are sure it is safe to increase your speed.

Pay attention to motorway signals.

172. If red lights on the overhead signals flash above your lane (there may also be a red X), you **MUST NOT** go beyond the signal in that lane. If red lights flash on a signal in the central reservation or a slip-road, you **MUST NOT** go beyond the signal in any lane.

173. All signals are there to protect you. Always do what they say. Remember – danger, such as drifting fog, may be there even if you cannot immediately see the cause.

Road studs and signs
174. To help drivers on motorways at night, there are amber-coloured studs marking the right-hand edge of the road, red studs marking the left-hand edge and green studs separating the slip-road from the motorway. White studs separate the lanes on the motorway.

175. On some motorways, direction signs are placed over the road. If you need to change lanes, do so in good time.

Fog
176. When driving in fog, obey the fog code (see Rule 58).

Road works
177. Take special care at road works (see Rules 147–148). One or more lanes may be closed to traffic and a lower speed limit may apply. Keep a safe distance from the vehicle in front (see Rule 57).

Obstructions
178. If anything that could be dangerous falls from your vehicle or any other vehicle, stop at the next emergency telephone to tell the police. Do not try to remove it yourself.

Stopping and parking
179. You **MUST NOT** stop except:
- in an emergency;
- when told to do so by the police, by an emergency sign or by flashing red light signals.

180. You **MUST NOT** park on:
- the carriageway;
- the slip-road;
- the hard shoulder;
- the central reservation.

181. You **MUST NOT** pick up or set down anyone on a slip-road or on any other part of the motorway.

182. You **MUST NOT** walk on the carriageway except in an emergency.

Breakdowns

183. If your vehicle develops a problem, leave the motorway at the next exit or pull into a service area. If you cannot do so, you should:

- try to stop near an emergency telephone (you will find them at one mile intervals along the hard shoulder);
- pull on to the hard shoulder and stop as far to the left as possible;
- switch on your hazard warning lights;
- keep your sidelights on if it is dark or visibility is poor;
- leave the vehicle by the left-hand door and ensure your passengers do the same (leave any animals inside);
- ensure passengers wait near the vehicle, but well away from the carriageway and hard shoulder, and that children are kept under control;
- walk to an emergency telephone (following the arrows on the posts at the back of the hard shoulder) – it is free to use and connects directly to the police. Give full details to the police – tell them if you are a woman travelling alone – and then return to your vehicle;
- wait near your vehicle but well away from the carriageway and hard shoulder. If you feel at risk, return to your vehicle by a left-hand door and lock all doors. Leave your vehicle again as soon as you feel the danger has passed.

If you cannot get your vehicle on to the hard shoulder:
- switch on your hazard warning lights;
- leave your vehicle only if you are sure you can safely get clear of the carriageway;
- if in doubt, remain in your vehicle wearing a seat belt until the emergency services arrive;
- do not attempt to place a warning triangle on the carriageway.

If you have a disability which prevents you from following the above advice:
- stay in your vehicle with all doors locked;
- switch on your hazard warning lights;

- display a 'Help' pennant or, if you have a car telephone, contact the emergency services.

Do not attempt even simple repairs and remember you **MUST NOT** try to cross the motorway.

184.   Before rejoining the carriageway, build-up speed on the hard shoulder and watch for a safe gap in the traffic.

LEAVING THE MOTORWAY

185.   Unless signs indicate that a lane leads directly off the motorway, you will leave the motorway by a slip-road on your left. Watch for the signs letting you know you are getting near your exit. If you are not already in the left-hand lane, move into it well before reaching your exit and stay in it. Signal left in good time and slow down as necessary.

186.   When leaving the motorway or using a link road between motorways, your speed may be higher than you think – 50 mph may feel like 30 mph. Check your speedometer and adjust your speed accordingly. Some slip-roads and link roads have sharp bends so you will need to slow down.

EXTRA RULES FOR CYCLISTS

CHOOSING AND MAINTAINING YOUR CYCLE

187.   Choose the right size of cycle for comfort and safety.

188.   Make sure that the:
- lights and reflectors are kept clean and in good working order;

- tyres are in good condition and inflated to the pressure recommended by the cycle manufacturer;
- brakes and gears are working correctly;
- chain is properly adjusted and oiled;
- saddle is adjusted to the correct height.

189. Fit a bell and use it when necessary to warn other road users, particularly blind and partially sighted pedestrians, that you are there.

Wear clothes which will help you to be seen.

SAFETY EQUIPMENT AND CLOTHING

190. Wear a cycle helmet which conforms to recognised safety standards. Choose appropriate clothes for cycling. Avoid long coats or other clothes which may get tangled in the chain or a wheel. Light-coloured or fluorescent clothing helps other road users see you in daylight and poor visibility.

191. At night you **MUST** use front and rear lights and a red rear reflector. Reflective material such as belts, arm and ankle bands, wheel reflectors and 'spacer' flags will also help you to be seen at night.

192. You **MUST** obey traffic signs and traffic light signals (see pages 54, 58 and 59). You **MUST NOT** cycle on the pavement.

193. Look all around before moving away from the kerb, turning or manoeuvring to make sure it is safe to do so. Then give a clear arm signal to show other road users what you intend to do.

194. Look well ahead for obstructions in the road, such as drains, pot-holes and parked cars so that you do not have to swerve suddenly to avoid them. Leave plenty of room when passing parked cars and watch out for doors being opened into your path.

195. Take care near road humps, narrowings and other traffic calming features. Do not ride along a drainage channel at the edge of the road to avoid such features.

196. Do not leave your cycle where it would endanger or obstruct other road users, for example lying on the pavement. Use cycle parking facilities where provided.

Road junctions
197. Watch out for vehicles turning in front of you from or into a side road. Do not overtake on the left of vehicles slowing down to turn left. Pay particular attention to long vehicles which need a lot of room to manoeuvre at corners and may have to move over to the right before turning left. Wait until they have completed the manoeuvre.

198. When turning right, check the traffic behind you, signal and when it is safe move to the centre of the road. Wait until there is a safe gap in traffic before completing the turn. It may be safer to wait on the left until there is a safe gap or to dismount and walk your cycle across the road.

Signal controlled junctions
199. Traffic signals also apply to cyclists. You **MUST NOT** cross the stop line across the road

when the lights are red. Some junctions have advanced stop lines which enable cyclists to position themselves ahead of other traffic. Where these are provided, use them.

Roundabouts

200.   Rules 123–128 set out the correct procedures at roundabouts but you may feel safer approaching in the left-hand lane and keeping to the left in the roundabout. If you do keep to the left, take extra care when cycling across exits and signal right to show you are not leaving. Watch out for vehicles crossing your path to leave or join the roundabout.

201.   Watch out for long vehicles on the roundabout as they need more space to manoeuvre. It may be safer to wait until they have cleared the roundabout.

202.   If you are unsure about using the roundabout, dismount and walk your cycle round on the pavement or verge.

Bus lanes

203.   You may only use a bus lane if the signs include a cycle symbol. Be very careful when overtaking a bus or leaving a bus lane as you will be entering a busier traffic flow.

Dual carriageways

204.   Take great care when crossing or turning on to a dual carriageway where there are no traffic light signals. Wait for safe gaps and cross each carriageway in turn. Remember that traffic on most dual carriageways travels quickly.

Cycle lanes and tracks

205.   Use cycle lanes and tracks wherever possible. They can make your journey safer and quicker.

206.   Cycle lanes are marked by either an unbroken or broken white line along the carriageway (see Rule 98). Keep within the lane and watch out for traffic emerging from side turnings.

207.   Cycle tracks are located away from the road. Where a cycle track is shared with a footpath, you **MUST** keep to the track intended for cyclists. Watch out for pedestrians, especially elderly people and people with disabilities, using the footpath or crossing the cycle track.

208. Cycle tracks on opposite sides of the road are sometimes linked by signalled crossings. If the crossing is provided for cyclists only, you may ride across but you **MUST NOT** cross until the green cycle symbol is showing. Do not ride across a Pelican crossing.

Safe riding
209. When cycling:

- keep both hands on the handlebars except when signalling or changing gear;
- keep both feet on the pedals;
- do not ride more than two abreast;
- ride in single file on cycle tracks and lanes, and on narrow roads when in traffic;
- do not ride close behind another vehicle;
- do not carry anything which will affect your balance or may get tangled up with your wheels or chain.

210. You **MUST NOT** carry a passenger unless your cycle has been built or adapted to carry one.

211. You **MUST NOT** ride under the influence of drink or drugs.

ANIMALS

GENERAL

212. Do not let your dog out on its own. Keep it on a short lead when taking it for a walk on or near a road or on a path shared with cyclists.

213. Keep animals under control in vehicles. Make sure they cannot distract you while you are driving. Do not let a dog out of a vehicle on to the road unless it is on a lead.

214. If you are herding animals, keep to the left of the road; if possible, send another person along the road to warn other road users, for example at bends and the brows of hills.

215. If you have to herd animals after dark, wear reflective clothing and ensure that white lights are carried at the front and red lights at the rear of the herd.

HORSE RIDERS

216. Before you take a horse on to a road, make sure you can control it. If you think that your horse will be nervous of traffic, always ride with other, less nervous, horses.

217. Make sure all tack fits well and is in good condition. Never ride a horse without a saddle or bridle.

218. Wear an approved safety helmet and fasten it securely – children under the age of 14 **MUST** do this. You should also wear boots or shoes with hard soles and heels.

219. If you have to ride at night, wear reflective clothing and make sure your horse has reflective bands on its legs above the fetlock joints. Carry lights which show white to the front and red to the rear.

220. Before riding off or turning, look behind you to make sure it is safe and then give a clear arm signal. When riding, keep to the left. If you are leading a horse, keep it to your left. In one-way streets, move in the direction of the traffic flow.

221. Never ride more than two abreast. Ride in single file on narrow roads.

222. You **MUST NOT** take a horse on to a footpath, pavement or cycle track. Use a bridle-path where possible.

223. Avoid roundabouts wherever possible. If you have to use them, keep to the left and watch out for vehicles crossing your path to leave or join the roundabout. Signal right when riding across exits to show you are not leaving. Signal left just before you leave the roundabout.

224. When riding:

- keep both hands on the reins unless you are signalling;
- keep both feet in the stirrups;
- do not carry another person;
- do not carry anything which might affect your balance or get tangled up with the reins;
- wear light-coloured or fluorescent clothing in daylight and reflective materials at night.

RAILWAY LEVEL CROSSINGS

GENERAL

225. A level crossing is where a road crosses railway lines. Approach and cross it with care. Never drive on to a crossing until the road is clear on the other side – do not drive 'nose to tail' over it. Never stop on or just after a crossing. Never park close to a crossing.

Take care at level crossings: do not zigzag round the barriers.

226. Most crossings have full or half barriers, traffic light signals with a steady amber light and twin flashing red stop lights (see page 54) and an audible alarm. You **MUST** stop behind the white line across the road when the lights come on. If you have already crossed the white line when the amber lights or audible alarm start, keep going.

227. If a train goes by and the red lights continue to flash or the audible alarm changes tone, you must wait. Another train will be passing soon. It is only safe to cross when the lights go off and any barriers open.

228. At crossings with half barriers, never zig-zag around the barriers. They are lowered because a train is approaching.

Railway telephones
229. If you are driving a large or slow-moving vehicle, or herding animals, you **MUST** obey any sign instructing you to use the railway telephone to obtain permission to cross. You **MUST** also telephone when clear of the crossing.

Accidents and breakdowns
230. If your vehicle breaks down, or if you have an accident on a crossing:

- get everyone out of the vehicle and clear of the crossing;
- if there is a railway telephone, use it immediately to tell the signal operator and follow the instructions you are given;
- if it is possible, and there is time before a train arrives, move the vehicle clear of the crossing. If the alarm sounds, or the amber light comes on, get clear of the crossing.

Crossings without signals
231. At crossings where there are gates or barriers but no lights, stop when they begin to close. Pedestrians should wait at the barrier or gate.

Unattended crossings with signals
232. Some unattended crossings with gates or barriers have 'STOP' signs and small red and green

lights. Do not cross when the red light is on as a train is approaching. Only cross if the green light is on. If crossing with a vehicle, open the gates or barriers on both sides of the crossing, then check that the green light is still on and cross quickly. Close the gates or barriers when you are clear of the crossing.

Unattended crossings without signals
233. Some crossings have gates but no attendant or traffic signals. At such crossings, stop, look both ways, listen and make sure no train is approaching. If there is a railway telephone, contact the signal operator to make sure it is safe to cross. If crossing with a vehicle, open the gates on both sides of the crossing, then check that no train is coming and cross quickly. When you have cleared the crossing, close both gates. Remember to inform the signal operator again when you are clear of the crossing.

Open crossings
234. At an open crossing with no gates, barriers, attendant or traffic lights, there will be a 'Give Way' sign. Look both ways, listen and make sure there is no train coming before you cross. Always 'Give Way' to trains – they cannot stop easily!

TRAMWAYS

GENERAL

235. You **MUST NOT** enter a road or lane reserved for trams. Diamond-shaped signs give instructions to tram drivers only.

236. Take extra care where trams (which can be up to 60 metres [196 ft] in length) run along the road. The area taken up by moving trams is often shown by tram lanes which will be marked by white lines or by a different type of road surface.

237. Take extra care where the track crosses from one side of the road to the other and where the road narrows and the tracks come close to the kerb. There will usually be separate traffic light signals giving instructions to tram drivers and to other traffic. Always give way to trams; do not try to race or overtake them.

238. Where tram stops have platforms, either in the middle or at the side of the road, you **MUST** follow the route shown by the road signs and markings. At stops without platforms, you **MUST NOT** drive between a tram and the left-hand kerb. If a tram is approaching a stop, look out for pedestrians, especially children, running to catch it.

239. You **MUST NOT** park your vehicle where it would get in the way of trams or where it would force other drivers to do so.

240. Cyclists and motorcyclists should take extra care when riding close to or crossing the tracks, especially if the rails are wet.

PEDESTRIANS

241. Where trams run through pedestrian areas, their path will be marked out by shallow kerbs, changes in the road surface or white lines. If the track is unfenced, you may cross at any point. Look both ways and when it is clear, walk straight across; do not walk along the track.

242. Use designated crossing places where provided. Some may have flashing amber lights to warn you that a tram is approaching. Do not start to cross the track when the lights are flashing. If you are already crossing when the lights start to flash, it will be safe to continue. Avoid treading on the rails.

SPEED LIMITS

Type of vehicle	Built-up areas*	Elsewhere			Motorways
		Single carriage-ways	Dual carriage-ways		
	MPH	MPH	MPH	MPH	MPH
Cars (including car derived vans and motorcycles)	30	60	70	70	70
Cars towing caravans or trailers (including car derived vans and motorcycles)	30	50	60	60	60
Buses and coaches (not exceeding 12 metres in overall length)	30	50	60	70	70
Goods vehicles (not exceeding 7.5 tonnes maximum laden weight)	30	50	60	70†	70†
Goods vehicles (exceeding 7.5 tonnes maximum laden weight)	30	40	50	60	60

These are the national speed limits and apply to all roads unless signs show otherwise.

* The 30 mph limit applies to all traffic on all roads in England and Wales (and Class C and unclassified roads in Scotland) with street lighting unless signs show otherwise.

† 60 if articulated or towing a trailer

53

LIGHT SIGNALS CONTROLLING TRAFFIC

RED means 'Stop'. Wait behind the stop line on the carriageway	RED AND AMBER also means 'Stop'. Do not pass through or start until GREEN shows	GREEN means you may go on if the way is clear. Take special care if you intend to turn left or right and give way to pedestrians who are crossing	AMBER means 'Stop' at the stop line. You may go on only if the AMBER appears after you have crossed the stop line or are so close to it that to pull up might cause an accident	A GREEN ARROW may be provided in addition to the full green signal if movement in a certain direction is allowed before or after the full green phase. If the way is clear you may go but only in the direction shown by the arrow. You may do this whatever other lights may be showing. White light signals may be provided for trams

FLASHING RED LIGHTS

Alternately flashing red lights mean YOU MUST STOP

At level crossings, lifting bridges, airfields, fire stations etc

MOTORWAY SIGNALS

Do not proceed further in this lane · Change lane · Reduced visibility ahead · Lane ahead closed

    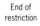

Temporary maximum speed limit and information message · Leave motorway at next exit · Temporary maximum speed limit · End of restriction

LANE CONTROL SIGNALS

Green arrow – lane available to traffic facing the sign. Red crosses – lane closed to traffic facing the sign. White diagonal arrow – change lanes in direction shown

SIGNALS BY AUTHORISED PERSONS

STOP

Traffic approaching from behind

Traffic approaching from the front

Traffic approaching from both front and behind

BECKONING TRAFFIC ON

Beckoning on traffic from the front

Beckoning on traffic from the side

Beckoning on traffic from behind

SIGNALS TO OTHER ROAD USERS

DIRECTION INDICATOR SIGNALS

 I intend to move out to the right or turn right

 I intend to move in to the left or turn left or stop on the left

BRAKE LIGHT SIGNALS

 I am slowing down or stopping

These signals should not be used except for the purposes described.

ARM SIGNALS

For use when direction indicator signals are not used; or when necessary to reinforce direction indicator signals and stop lights. Also for use by pedal cyclists and those in charge of horses.

 I intend to move out to the right or turn right

 I intend to move in to the left or turn left

 I intend to slow down or stop
This signal is particularly important at Zebra crossings to let other road users, including pedestrians, know that you are slowing down or stopping

ARM SIGNALS TO PERSONS CONTROLLING TRAFFIC

I want to go straight on

I want to turn left

I want to turn right

TRAFFIC SIGNS

SIGNS GIVING ORDERS

These signs are mostly circular and those with red circles are mostly prohibitive.

Entry to 20 mph zone

End of 20 mph zone

School crossing patrol

Maximum speed

National speed limit applies

Stop and give way

Give way to traffic on major road

No vehicles except bicycles being pushed

No entry for vehicular traffic

No right turn

No left turn

No U-turns

No overtaking

Give way to oncoming vehicles

Give priority to vehicles from opposite direction

No motor vehicles

No motor vehicles except solo motorcycles, scooters or mopeds

Manually operated temporary 'STOP' sign

Up to 31.12.96: No vehicles with over 12 seats except regular scheduled, school and works buses. From 1.1.97: No buses (over 8 seats)

No cycling

No pedestrians

No horses

No vehicle or combination of vehicles over length shown

No vehicles over height shown

No vehicles over width shown

WEAK BRIDGE

No vehicles over maximum gross weight shown (in tonnes)

No goods vehicles over maximum gross weight shown (in tonnes)

No stopping (Clearway)

Permit holders only

Parking restricted to permit holders

URBAN CLEARWAY
Monday to Friday
am 8-9.30   pm 4.30-6.30

No stopping during times shown except for as long as necessary to set down or pick up passengers

Plates below some signs qualify their message

End

End of restriction

Except for loading

Exception for loading/unloading goods

Except buses

Exception for regular scheduled school and works buses

Except for access

Exception for access to premises and land adjacent to the road where there is no alternative route

58

Signs with blue circles but no red border mostly give positive instruction.

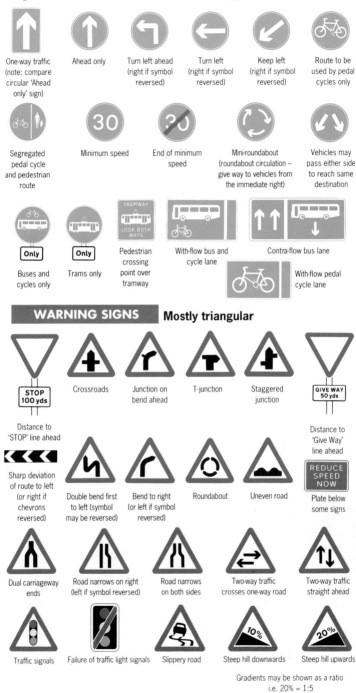

One-way traffic (note: compare circular 'Ahead only' sign)

Ahead only

Turn left ahead (right if symbol reversed)

Turn left (right if symbol reversed)

Keep left (right if symbol reversed)

Route to be used by pedal cycles only

Segregated pedal cycle and pedestrian route

Minimum speed

End of minimum speed

Mini-roundabout (roundabout circulation – give way to vehicles from the immediate right)

Vehicles may pass either side to reach same destination

Buses and cycles only

Trams only

Pedestrian crossing point over tramway

With-flow bus and cycle lane

Contra-flow bus lane

With-flow pedal cycle lane

WARNING SIGNS   Mostly triangular

STOP 100 yds

Distance to 'STOP' line ahead

Crossroads

Junction on bend ahead

T-junction

Staggered junction

GIVE WAY 50 yds

Distance to 'Give Way' line ahead

Sharp deviation of route to left (or right if chevrons reversed)

Double bend first to left (symbol may be reversed)

Bend to right (or left if symbol reversed)

Roundabout

Uneven road

REDUCE SPEED NOW

Plate below some signs

Dual carriageway ends

Road narrows on right (left if symbol reversed)

Road narrows on both sides

Two-way traffic crosses one-way road

Two-way traffic straight ahead

Traffic signals

Failure of traffic light signals

Slippery road

Steep hill downwards

Steep hill upwards

Gradients may be shown as a ratio i.e. 20% = 1:5

Warning signs – continued

Children going to or from school

Elderly people (or blind or disabled as shown) crossing road

Pedestrians in road ahead

Pedestrian crossing

Cycle route ahead

Patrol

School crossing patrol ahead (some signs have amber lights which flash when children are crossing)

Side winds

Hump bridge

Worded warning sign

Risk of ice

Risk of grounding

Light signals ahead at level crossing, airfield or bridge

Level crossing with barrier or gate ahead

Level crossing without barrier or gate ahead

Level crossing without barrier

Trams crossing ahead

Cattle

Wild animals

Wild horses or ponies

Accompanied horses or ponies

Quayside or river bank

Opening or swing bridge ahead

Low-flying aircraft or sudden aircraft noise

Falling or fallen rocks

Available width of headroom indicated

Safe height 16·6″

Overhead electric cable; plate indicates maximum height of vehicles which can pass safely

1 mile

Distance to tunnel

Humps for ½ mile

Distance over which road humps extend

Hidden dip

Other danger; plate indicates nature of danger

Soft verges for 2 miles

Soft verges

DIRECTION SIGNS   **Mostly rectangular**

Signs on motorways – blue backgrounds

At a junction leading directly into a motorway (junction number may be shown on a black background)

On approaches to junctions (junction number on black background)

Route confirmatory sign after junction

Downward pointing arrows mean 'Get in lane'
The left-hand lane leads to a different destination from the other lanes

The panel with the sloping arrow indicates the destinations which can be reached by leaving the motorway at the next junction

Signs on primary routes – green backgrounds

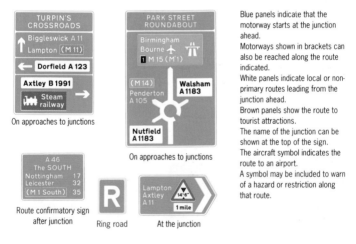

On approaches to junctions

On approaches to junctions

Blue panels indicate that the motorway starts at the junction ahead.

Motorways shown in brackets can also be reached along the route indicated.

White panels indicate local or non-primary routes leading from the junction ahead.

Brown panels show the route to tourist attractions.

The name of the junction can be shown at the top of the sign.

The aircraft symbol indicates the route to an airport.

A symbol may be included to warn of a hazard or restriction along that route.

Route confirmatory sign after junction   Ring road   At the junction

Signs on non-primary and local routes – black borders

On approaches to junctions

Green panels indicate that the primary route starts at the junction ahead. Route numbers on a blue background show the direction to a motorway. Route numbers on a green background show the direction to a primary route.

At the junction

Direction to toilets with access for the disabled

Other direction signs

Wrest Park ›
Ancient monument in the care of English Heritage

300yds ›
Direction to camping and caravan site

300yds ›
Picnic site

Zoo ›
Tourist attraction

HR
Holiday route

(A33) (M1) →
Advisory route for lorries

Council Offices Public Library ››
Route for pedestrians

‹ Northtown
Diversion route

□ ▲ ◆ ○
Symbols showing emergency diversion route for motorway traffic

Marton 3 ›
Recommended route for pedal cycles to place shown

P Saturday only ›
Direction to a car park

INFORMATION SIGNS   All rectangular

M 23
Start of motorway and point from which motorway regulations apply

ONE WAY ←
One-way street (Sign for pedestrians)

Priority over oncoming vehicles
Traffic has priority over oncoming vehicles

T
No through road

H A & E not 24 hrs
Hospital ahead with Accident and Emergency facilities

End of motorway

P
Parking place for towed caravans

Low bridge 2 miles ahead
4.4 m 14'6"
Advance warning of restriction or prohibition ahead

GOOD FOOD
Puddleworth services ½m
Petrol 45p
Motorway service area sign showing the operator's name

i Tourist information
Tourist information point

Recommended route for pedal cycles

Except buses ← ↑ ↑ →
Appropriate traffic lanes at junction ahead

'Countdown' markers at exit from motorway (each bar represents 100 yards to the exit). Green-backed markers may be used on primary routes and white-backed markers with red bars on the approaches to concealed level crossings

Meter ZONE
Mon - Fri 8.30 am - 6.30 pm
Saturday 8.30 am - 1.30 pm
Entrance to controlled parking zone

Zone ENDS
End of controlled parking zone

local cycle taxi
With-flow bus lane ahead

Bus lane ←
Bus lane on road at junction ahead

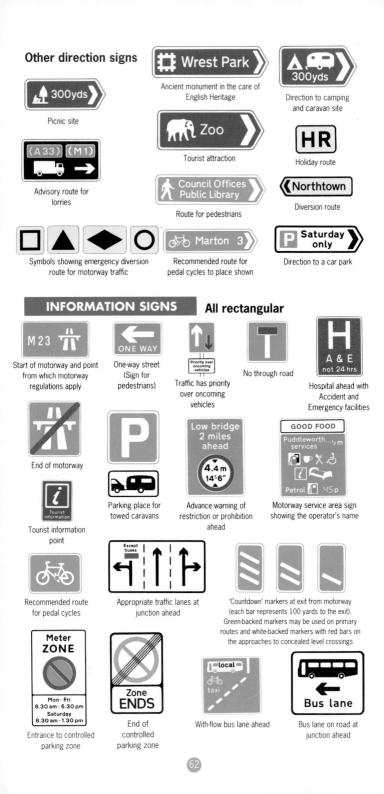

62

ROAD WORKS SIGNS

Road works

Loose chippings

Road works
1 mile ahead

End of road works
and any temporary
restrictions

Temporary hazard
at road works

Temporary lane closure
(the number and position
of arrows and red bars
may be varied according
to lanes open and closed)

Lane restrictions at
road works ahead

One lane
crossover at
contraflow road
works

Signs used on the back of slow-moving or
stationary vehicles warning of a lane closed
ahead by a works vehicle. There are no cones
on the road.

Slow-moving or stationary
works vehicle blocking a traffic
lane. Pass in the direction
shown by the arrow.

ROAD MARKINGS

ACROSS THE CARRIAGEWAY

Stop line at signals or police control

Stop line at 'STOP' sign

Give way to traffic on major road

Give way to traffic from the right
at a roundabout

Give way to traffic from the right
at a mini-roundabout

Stop line for pedestrians
at a level crossing

ALONG THE EDGE OF THE CARRIAGEWAY

Waiting restrictions

Waiting restrictions indicated by yellow lines apply to the carriageway, pavement and verge. You may stop to load and unload or while passengers board or alight unless there are also loading restrictions as described below. The times at which the restrictions apply are shown on nearby plates or on entry signs to controlled parking zones. If no days are shown on the signs, the restrictions are in force every day including Sundays and Bank Holidays.

Between now and January 1999 the yellow line system is being simplified.

YELLOW LINES CAN ONLY GIVE A GUIDE TO THE RESTRICTIONS IN FORCE AND TIME PLATES OR ZONE ENTRY SIGNS MUST BE CONSULTED.

No waiting
at any time

No waiting
during times
shown on sign

Alternative ways of indicating that
waiting is limited to the times and
duration shown

ON THE KERB OR AT THE EDGE OF THE CARRIAGEWAY

Loading restrictions

Yellow marks on the kerb or at the edge of the carriageway indicate that loading or unloading is prohibited at the times shown on the nearby black and white plates. If no days are indicated on the signs the restrictions are in force every day including Sundays and Bank Holidays.

ALWAYS CHECK THE TIMES SHOWN ON THE PLATES.

Lengths of road reserved for vehicles loading and unloading are indicated by a white 'bay' marking with the words 'LOADING ONLY' and a sign with the white on blue 'trolley' symbol. This sign also shows whether loading and unloading is restricted to goods vehicles and the times at which the bay can be used. If no times or days are shown it may be used at any time. Vehicles may not park here if they are not loading or unloading.

No loading or
unloading at any time

No loading or unloading
at the times shown

Loading bay

Double white lines
See Rules 84 and 85

Hazard
warning line
See Rule 83

Lane line
See Rule 87

Centre line

Diagonal stripes
See Rule 86

Edge line

OTHER ROAD MARKINGS

— SCHOOL — KEEP — CLEAR —

Keep entrance clear of stationary vehicles, even if picking up or setting down children

Warning of 'Give Way'
just ahead

Parking space reserved
for vehicles named

See Rule 140

See Rule 97

KEEP

CLEAR

CITY | A 3 | YORK ST

Box junction
See Rule 113

Do not block entrance
to side road

Indication of traffic lanes

Note: Although *The Highway Code* shows many of the signs commonly in use, a comprehensive explanation of our signing system is given in the Department's booklet *Know Your Traffic Signs*, which is on sale at booksellers. The booklet also illustrates and explains the vast majority of signs the road user is likely to encounter. The signs illustrated in *The Highway Code* are not all drawn to the same scale. In Wales, bilingual versions of some signs are used. Some older designs of signs may still be seen on the roads.

VEHICLE MARKINGS

HEAVY GOODS VEHICLE REAR MARKINGS

Motor vehicles over 7500 kilograms maximum gross weight and trailers over 3500 kilograms maximum gross weight

School bus (displayed in front or rear window of bus or coach)

Left

Right

LONG VEHICLE

LONG VEHICLE

or

LONG VEHICLE

The vertical markings are also required to be fitted to builders' skips placed in the road, commercial vehicles or combinations longer than 13 metres (optional on combinations between 11 and 13 metres)

HAZARD WARNING PLATES

Certain tank vehicles carrying dangerous goods must display hazard information panels

2YE
1089
Newtown-on-Moors
(0123) 45678

FLAMMABLE LIQUID

The panel illustrated is for flammable liquid. Diamond symbols indicating other risks include:

COMPRESSED GAS

The above panel will be displayed by vehicles carrying certain dangerous goods in packages

Non-flammable compressed gas

TOXIC

OXIDIZING AGENT

!

RADIOACTIVE

SPONTANEOUSLY COMBUSTIBLE

CORROSIVE

Toxic substance

Oxidizing substance

Multi-loads

Radioactive substance

Spontaneously combustible substance

Corrosive substance

PROJECTION MARKERS

Side marker

End marker

Both required when load or equipment (eg crane jib) overhangs front or rear by more than two metres

THE ROAD USER AND THE LAW

ROAD TRAFFIC LAW

This section deals with some of the important points of law which affect road safety. It is not intended to be a comprehensive guide. For the precise wording of the law, please refer to the various Acts and Regulations (as amended) indicated in the margin. A list of abbreviations used is given below.

Most of the provisions apply on all roads throughout Great Britain, although there are some exceptions. The definition of a road in England and Wales is 'any highway and any other road to which the public has access and includes bridges over which a road passes.' In Scotland, there is a similar definition which is extended to include any way over which the public have a right of passage. It is important to note that references to 'road' therefore generally include footpaths, bridle-ways and cycle tracks. In most cases, the law will apply to them and there may be additional rules for particular paths or ways. Some serious driving offences, including drink-driving offences, also apply to other public places, for example public car parks.

Road Vehicles (Construction & Use) Regulations 1986	**CUR**
Functions of Traffic Wardens Order 1970	**FTWO**
Highways Act (1835 or 1980, as indicated)	**HA**
Horses (Protective Headgear for Young Riders) Regulations 1992	**H(PHYR)R**
Motor Cycles (Protective Helmets) Regulations 1980	**MC(PH)R**
Motorways Traffic (England & Wales) Regulations 1982	**ME(E&W)R**
Motorways Traffic (England & Wales) (Amendment) Regulations 1992	**MT(E&W)(A)R**
Motorways Traffic (Scotland) Regulations 1964	**MT(S)R**
Motor Vehicles (Driving Licences) Regulations 1987	**MV(DL)R**
Motor Vehicles (Wearing of Seat Belts) Regulations 1982	**MV(WSB)R**
Motor Vehicles (Wearing of Seat Belts by Children) Regulations 1982	**MV(WSBC)R**
Motor Vehicles (Wearing of Seat Belts by Children in Rear Seats) Regulations 1989	**MV(WSBCRS)R**
Motor Vehicles (Wearing of Seat Belts in Rear Seats by Adults) Regulations 1991	**MV(WSBRSA)R**
Pedal Cycles (Construction & Use) Regulations 1983	**PCUR**
'Pelican' Pedestrian Crossing Regulations & General Directions 1987	**PPCRGD**
Public Passenger Vehicles Act 1981	**PPVA**
Roads (Scotland) Act 1984	**R(S)A**
Road Traffic Act 1988	**RTA**
Road Traffic Regulation Act 1984	**RTRA**
Road Vehicles Lighting Regulations 1989	**RVLR**
Road Vehicles (Registration & Licensing) Regulations 1971	**RV(R&L)R**
Traffic Signs Regulations & General Directions 1994	**TSRGD**
Vehicles (Excise) Act 1971	**VEA**
'Zebra' Pedestrian Crossings Regulations 1971	**ZPCR**

[E&W = England and Wales; S = Scotland]

A TO DRIVERS OF MOTOR VEHICLES

1. DOCUMENTS: TAX, LICENCE, INSURANCE, ETC
You **MUST** have:

RTA Sect 87

- a **valid driving licence**;

VEA Sects 1 & 12(4)

- a **current vehicle excise licence (tax disc)** which must be displayed on the vehicle;

RTA Sect 143

- valid third party **insurance** covering your use of the vehicle;

RTA Sects 45, 47, 49 & 53

- a current **test certificate (MOT)** if your vehicle is over the prescribed age limit.

2. YOUR VEHICLE

CUR No 100

The law requires that the condition of your vehicle, any trailer it is drawing, its load, and the number of passengers and the way in which they are carried are such that they do not involve danger of injury to yourself or others.

There are more detailed regulations which require the different parts of your vehicle to be kept in good condition and working order. These include **brakes, steering, lights, windscreens and windows, exhaust, seat belts and fittings, speedometer and horn**.

CUR No 27

Tyres MUST have a continuous tread depth of at least 1.6 mm on cars, light vans and light trailers (1 mm for other vehicles) across the centre three-quarters of the width. They **MUST** also be properly inflated and free from cuts and other defects.

RVLR Nos 23 & 27

Headlights MUST be properly adjusted to prevent dazzling oncoming traffic.

CUR Nos 30 & 34

Windscreens and windows MUST be free from obstruction to vision, and **MUST** be kept clean.

3. WEARING OF SEAT BELTS

RTA Sect 14
RTA(A)R No 3105
MV(WSBCFS)R No 31
MV(WSB)R No 176

You and your passengers **MUST** wear a seat belt in the front and (if fitted) the rear of the vehicle, unless you are exempt. Exemptions include the holders of medical exemption certificates, people making local deliveries in a vehicle designed or adapted for that purpose, and children in the rear of taxis with partitions. (See table in Rule 40 of the Code.)

RTA Sect 15
MV(WSBCFS)R No 31
MV(WSB)R No 176

It is the driver's legal responsibility to ensure that children under 14 years comply with the law.

4. FITNESS TO DRIVE

RTA Sect 94

You **MUST** report to the licensing authority any health condition likely to affect your driving.

RTA Sect 96
MV(DL)R No 20(1)(c)
& Sch 4

Your eyesight **MUST** be up to the standard required for the driving test (see Rule 34 of the Code) at all times when you drive.

Drinking and driving
You **MUST NOT**:

RTA Sect 4

- drive under the influence of drink or drugs;

- drive with a breath alcohol level higher than 35 µg/100 ml (equivalent to a blood alcohol level of 80 mg/100 ml).

RTA Sects 5 & 11(2)

5. ON THE ROAD
You **MUST** comply with:
- maximum speed limits (see page 53) or any special speed limit for your vehicle;
- amber and red 'STOP' signals, traffic signs giving orders, double white lines and yellow road markings;

- the directions of a police officer or traffic warden controlling traffic.

RTRA Sects 81, 84, 86, 89 and Sch 6
TSRGD Nos 7, 23(1), 34(1) and Sch 2
PPCRGD No 16
RTRA Sects 1, 6 & 9
RTA Sect 35
FTWO No 3

You **MUST NOT**:
- drive dangerously;
- drive without due care and attention or without reasonable consideration for other road users;
- drive on a footway, footpath, bridle-way or cycle track at any time, or a bus or cycle lane during its hours of operation.

RTA Sect 2
RTA Sect 3

HA 1835 Sect 72
RTRA Sects 1, 6 & 9
RTA Sects 21 & 34
R(S)A Sect 129(5)

6. PEDESTRIAN CROSSINGS
Zebra and Pelican crossings
Pedestrians have precedence on the carriageway within the limits of a Zebra crossing, and on a Pelican crossing when the signal to cross is lit up. You **MUST** give way to pedestrians on a Zebra crossing or when an amber light is flashing on a Pelican crossing.

ZPCR No 8
PPCRGD No 17

The carriageway on the approach to a Zebra or Pelican crossing is normally marked by zigzag lines. In this area you **MUST NOT**:
- overtake the moving motor vehicle nearest the crossing;
- overtake the leading vehicle which has stopped to give way to a pedestrian.

ZPCR No 10
PPCRGD No 19

School crossing patrols
You **MUST** stop when signalled to do so by a school crossing patrol exhibiting a 'STOP' for children sign.

RTRA Sect 28

7. DRIVING AT NIGHT OR IN REDUCED VISIBILITY
You **MUST**:
- ensure your front and rear side lights and rear registration plate lights are lit at night;
- use headlights at night on all unlit roads and those where the street lights are more than 185 metres (600ft) apart;
- use headlights when visibility is seriously reduced.

RVLR No 24
RV(R&L)R No 19
RVLR No 25

RVLR No 25

You **MUST NOT**:
- use headlights in a way which would dazzle or discomfort other road users;
- use front or rear fog lights unless visibility is seriously reduced;
- sound your horn at night (11.30 pm to 7 am) in a built-up area.

RVLR No 27

RVLR No 27

CUR No 99

8. WAITING AND PARKING

There are a number of places where the law specifically forbids you to let your vehicle stand. The most important of these are listed in Rules 138, 139 and 141 of the Code.

RTA Sect 22
CUR No 103

In addition there is a more general legal requirement that you **MUST NOT** park on the road in such a way that your vehicle or trailer is likely to cause danger to other road users or an unnecessary obstruction. Examples of places in which you are likely to be committing an offence are in Rule 140 of the Code.

9. PROVIDING INFORMATION TO THE POLICE

RTA Sect 163
RTA Sects 164 & 165

You **MUST** stop your vehicle when required to do so by a uniformed police officer, who may require you to produce documents including your driving licence, certificate of insurance and test certificate (MOT) for examination. If you are not carrying them with you, you may select a police station at which you can produce them within seven days.

10. ACCIDENTS

RTA Sect 170

If you are involved in an accident which causes damage or injury to any other person, or other vehicle, or any animal (horse, cattle, ass, mule, sheep, pig, goat or dog) not in your vehicle, or roadside property;

You **MUST**:

- stop;
- give your own and the vehicle owner's name and address and the registration number of the vehicle to anyone having reasonable grounds for requiring them;
- if you do not give your name and address at the time of the accident, report the accident to the police as soon as reasonably practicable, and in any case within 24 hours.

If any other person is injured and you do not produce your insurance certificate at the time of the accident to the police or to anyone who with reasonable grounds has requested it, you **MUST** also:

- report the accident to the police as soon as possible, and in any case within 24 hours;
- produce your insurance certificate to the police either when reporting the accident or within seven days at any police station you select.

B TO MOTORCYCLISTS AND MOPED RIDERS

Most of the requirements of the law relating to drivers of motor vehicles also apply to you.

In addition you **MUST**:

MC(PH)R
CUR 57

RTA Sect 23

- wear an approved safety helmet on all journeys;
- ensure that your exhaust system and silencer are of an approved type;
- carry no more than one passenger on a motorcycle.

Learners **MUST** comply with the requirements in Rule 37 of the Code.

Pillion passengers MUST:
- wear an approved type of safety helmet;
- sit astride the cycle on a proper seat securely fitted behind the driver's seat and with proper rests for the feet.

MC(PH)R
CUR No 102

C MOTORWAY DRIVING

Motorways **MUST NOT** be used by pedestrians, holders of provisional ordinary licences, pedal cycles, motorcycles under 50cc, invalid carriages not exceeding 254 kg unladen weight, certain slow-moving vehicles carrying oversized loads (except by special permission), agricultural vehicles and animals.

HA 1980 Sects 16, 17 & Sch 4
MT(E&W)R No 4
MT(E&W)(A)R
R(S)A Sects 7 & 8
MT(S)R No 10

You **MUST**:
- drive on the carriageways only;

- observe one-way driving on the carriageways;

- observe maximum speed limits (see page 53) or any special speed limit for your vehicle;
- observe flashing red signals when displayed over your lane or at the side of the carriageway;
- keep any animals in the vehicle or (in an emergency) under proper control on the verge.

MT(E&W)R No 5
MT(S)R No 4
MT(E&W)R No 6
MT(S)R No 5
RTRA Sects 17, 86 & Sch 6
RTA Sect 36
TSRGD No 34(4)
MT(E&W)R No 14
MT(S)R No 12

You **MUST NOT**:
- drive in reverse on the carriageway;

- stop on the carriageway; or on the hard shoulder (except in an emergency); or on the central reservation or verge.

MT(E&W)R No 8
MT(S)R No 7
MT(E&W)R
Nos 7(1), 9 & 10
MT(S)R Nos 6(1), 8 & 9

Motorways: right-hand lanes
You **MUST NOT** use the right-hand lane of a motorway with three or more lanes (except in prescribed circumstances) if you are driving
- any vehicle drawing a trailer;
- a goods vehicle with a maximum laden weight over 7.5 tonnes;
- a bus or coach longer than 12 metres.

MT(E&W)R No 12
MT(S)R No 10A

D TO PEDESTRIANS

You have precedence over other road users when you are on the carriageway within the limits of a Zebra crossing, and on a Pelican crossing when the signal to cross is lit. But you **MUST NOT** loiter on a pedestrian crossing.

ZPCR
PPCRGD

You **MUST NOT**:
- walk on motorways or their slip-roads;

- walk on the carriageway when directed not to do so by a police officer or traffic warden controlling traffic;
- hold on to or get on a moving motor vehicle or trailer.

RTRA Sect 17
MT(E&W)R No 15
RTA Sect 37

RTA Sects 25 & 26

E TO PEDAL CYCLISTS

You **MUST** obey the same rules as apply to drivers at pedestrian crossings and school crossing patrols (see A.6 on page 69).

In addition you **MUST**:

PCUR Nos 7–10
RVLR Nos 18, 23 & 24
RVLR No 24

- ensure that your brakes are efficient;
- at night, ensure your front and rear lights are lit and that your cycle has an efficient red rear reflector;
- at night, if you are wheeling your cycle or are stationary without lights, keep as close as possible to the nearside edge of the road;

RTA Sect 163

- stop when required to do so by a uniformed police officer or traffic warden.

You **MUST NOT**:

RTA Sect 28
RTA Sect 29

RTA Sect 30
HA 1835 Sect 72
R(S)A Sect 129(5)
RTA Sect 22

RTA Sect 24

RTA Sect 26

- ride dangerously;
- ride without due care and attention or without reasonable consideration for other road users;
- ride under the influence of drink or drugs;
- ride on a footway or footpath unless there is a right to do so;
- leave your cycle on any road in such a way that it is likely to cause danger to other road users, or where waiting is prohibited;
- carry a passenger on a bicycle not constructed or adapted to carry more than one person;
- hold on to a moving motor vehicle or trailer.

F TO HORSE RIDERS

You **MUST NOT** deliberately ride, lead or drive your horse:

HA 1835 Sect 72

R(S)A Sect 129(5)

H(PHYR)R

- on a footpath by the side of any road made or set apart for the use of pedestrians (England & Wales);
- on a footway, footpath or cycle track unless there is a right to do so (Scotland).

Children under 14 **MUST** wear a properly secured approved safety helmet.

Parliament has set the maximum penalties for road traffic offences and within these maxima it is for the courts to decide what sentence to impose according to the circumstances. The maximum penalties for each offence are intended to reflect the seriousness of the offence.

The penalty table on page 74 indicates some of the main offences, and the associated penalties. (There are a wide range of other more specific offences which, for the sake of simplicity, are not shown here.)

The operation of the penalty points and disqualification system is described below.

PENALTY POINTS AND DISQUALIFICATIONS

1. For any offence which carries penalty points the courts have a discretionary power to order a period of disqualification. In the case of obligatory disqualification, the courts must disqualify for a minimum period of 12 months. For repeat offenders this may be longer. For example, a second drink-drive offence within 10 years will result in a minimum of three years disqualification.

2. The penalty point system is intended to deter drivers from unsafe driving. The court must order penalty points to be endorsed on the licence according to the fixed number or within the range set by Parliament. The accumulation of penalty points acts as a warning to drivers that they risk disqualification if further offences are committed. Any driver who accumulates 12 or more points within a three-year period must be disqualified for a minimum period of six months and for a longer period if the driver has previously been disqualified.

OTHER CONSEQUENCES OF OFFENDING

3. In addition to the penalties a court may decide to impose, the cost of insurance is likely to rise considerably following conviction for a serious driving offence – in line with the increased risk of having an accident which insurance companies consider attaches to such drivers.

4. Drivers convicted of drinking and driving twice within 10 years, or once if they are over two and a half times the legal limit, or those who refuse to give a specimen, also have to satisfy the Driver and Vehicle Licensing Agency's Medical Branch that they do not have an alcohol problem and are otherwise fit to drive before their licence is returned at the end of their period of disqualification.

PENALTY TABLE

Offence	Maximum penalties			
	IMPRISONMENT	FINE	DISQUALIFICATION	PENALTY POINTS
*Causing death by dangerous driving	10 years	Unlimited	Obligatory – 2 years minimum	3–11 (if exceptionally not disqualified)
*Dangerous driving	2 years	Unlimited	Obligatory	3–11 (if exceptionally not disqualified)
Causing death by careless driving under the influence of drink or drugs	10 years	Unlimited	Obligatory – 2 years minimum	3–11 (if exceptionally not disqualified)
Careless and inconsiderate driving	–	£2,500	Discretionary	3–9
Driving while unfit through drink or drugs or with excess alcohol; or failing to provide a specimen for analysis	6 months	£5,000	Obligatory	3–11 (if exceptionally not disqualified)
Failing to stop after an accident or failing to report an accident	6 months	£5,000	Discretionary	5–10
Driving when disqualified	6 months (12 months in Scotland)	£5,000	Discretionary	6
Driving after refusal or revocation of licence on medical grounds	6 months	£5,000	Discretionary	3–6
Driving without insurance	–	£5,000	Discretionary	6–8
Driving otherwise than in accordance with a licence	–	£1,000	Discretionary	3–6
Speeding	–	£1,000 (£2,500 for motorway offences)	Discretionary	3–6 or 3 (fixed penalty)
Traffic light offences	–	£1,000	Discretionary	3
No MOT certificate	–	£1,000	–	–
Seat belt offences	–	£500	–	–
Dangerous cycling	–	£2,500	–	–
Careless cycling	–	£1,000	–	–
Failing to identify driver of a vehicle	–	£1,000	Discretionary	3

*Where a court disqualifies a person on conviction for one of these offences, it must order an extended retest – about twice as long as the ordinary driving test. The courts also have discretion to order a retest for any other offence which carries penalty points: an extended retest where disqualification is obligatory, and an ordinary test where disqualification is not obligatory

VEHICLE SECURITY

Over 2.5 million cars are broken into or stolen each year. That is one every 13 seconds.

A stolen car can mean having to walk home late at night. It can mean weeks of delay sorting out insurance, extra expense getting into work, loss of personal possessions, and losing your no-claims bonus.

So when you leave your vehicle always:
- Remove the ignition key and engage the steering lock.
- Lock the car, even if you only leave it for a few minutes.
- Close the windows **completely** – even the smallest gap is asking for trouble. But **never** leave children or pets in an unventilated car.
- Take all contents with you, or lock them in the boot. Remember, for all a thief knows a carrier bag may contain valuables. Never leave vehicle documents in the car.

For extra security fit an anti-theft device such as an alarm or immobiliser. If you are buying a new car it is a good idea to check the level of built-in security features. And it is well worthwhile having your registration number etched on all your car windows. This is a cheap and effective deterrent to professional thieves.

FIRST AID ON THE ROAD

For those with no first aid training.

DANGER – Deal with threatened danger or you and the casualties may be killed. FURTHER COLLISIONS and FIRE are the dangers in a road accident.

Action:
If possible warn other traffic. Switch off the engine. Impose a 'No Smoking' ban.

Obtaining further help:
Send a bystander to call an ambulance as soon as possible; state the exact location of the accident and the numbers of vehicles and casualties involved.

People remaining in vehicles:
Casualties remaining in vehicles should not be moved unless further danger is threatened.

If breathing has stopped:
Remove any obvious obstruction in the mouth. Keep the head tilted backwards as far as possible – breathing may begin and the colour may improve. If not, pinch the casualty's nostrils together and blow into the mouth until the chest rises; withdraw, then repeat regularly once every four seconds until the casualty can breathe unaided.

If unconscious and breathing:
Movement may further damage an injured back, so only move if in danger. If breathing becomes difficult or stops, treat as above.

If bleeding is present:
Apply firm hand pressure over the wound, preferably using some clean material, without pressing on any foreign body in the wound. Secure a pad with a bandage or length of cloth. Raise limb to lessen the bleeding, providing it is not broken.

Reassurance:
The casualty may be shocked but prompt treatment will minimise this; reassure confidently; avoid unnecessary movement; keep the casualty comfortable and prevent them getting cold; ensure they are not left alone.

Give the casualty NOTHING to drink.

Carry a first aid kit. Learn first aid from a qualified organisation, such as the St John Ambulance Association and Brigade, St Andrew's Ambulance Association, the British Red Cross Society or any other suitably qualified body.

THE THEORY OF SAFE AND RESPONSIBLE DRIVING

Additional information for

the theory element of the

Driving Test

Note: This advice is not part of the Highway Code and does not have the legal status of the Code between pages 3 and 52 (see introduction)

THE THEORY OF SAFE AND RESPONSIBLE DRIVING

CONTENTS

DRIVING SAFELY

More than 90 per cent of accidents are caused by a driver or rider making a mistake. You need to be fully alert at all times – don't allow yourself to be distracted. Try to be aware of all that is happening around you.

Anyone can make a mistake. There is no such thing as a perfect driver.

1.   Be particularly careful if you are a new driver. Statistics show that the 17 to 25-year-old age group and those who have recently passed a test are more likely to be involved in a fatal or serious accident.

2.   Seeing something isn't the same as being aware of it. You need to judge the degree of risk. A pedestrian on the pavement may
- stay where they are – no hazard at all
- be looking the other way and about to run into the road – a serious hazard

Try to judge what pedestrians and other road users might do.

3.   Being prepared for the unexpected improves your safety. Be ready for difficult situations – the road being blocked beyond a blind bend, for instance.

4.   Adapt your driving to the type of road. Take particular care on roads with junctions.
- slow down
- be prepared for vehicles pulling out

In side streets and country lanes where there may be unmarked junctions, proceed cautiously – nobody has priority at an unmarked junction.

5.   Don't treat speed limits as a target. It won't always be safe to drive at that limit. Always take the road and traffic conditions into account.

6.   Position yourself sensibly on the road. On right-hand bends for instance, keeping a position to the left will
- improve your view of the road
- help avoid the risk of colliding with traffic coming in the opposite direction.

7. Choose an appropriate place to manoeuvre. If you need to turn your car around, wait until you find a safe place. Don't reverse or turn round in busy roads. Find a quiet side road or drive round a block of side streets.

8. Driving safely needs all your concentration. Avoid distractions such as listening to loud music (which can mask other sounds) and don't try to do other things at the same time such as reading maps or using mobile phones.

9. Don't drink then drive. Alcohol will
• reduce co-ordination
• slow down reactions
• affect judgement of speed
Alcohol takes time to leave the body; you might still be unfit to drive the following morning. If you are going to drink, use public transport.

BE CAREFUL AND CONSIDERATE OF OTHER ROAD USERS

Don't drive aggressively. Try to be understanding if another driver causes a problem.

10. If someone is behaving badly on the road, don't get involved. If you feel angry, pull over and calm down.

11. If a vehicle behind you is trying to overtake but can't, take no action. Keep to a steady course and within the speed limit. Pull over if it is safe to do so and let the vehicle pass. Never obstruct drivers who wish to overtake. Speeding up or driving unpredictably while someone is overtaking you can be very dangerous.

12. Never overtake a vehicle indicating right. Even if you believe the signal should have been cancelled, don't take a risk. Wait for the signal to be cancelled.

13. If a vehicle pulls out into your path at a junction, slow down and hold back to allow it to get clear. Don't over-react by driving up too close behind it.

14. When following other vehicles leave enough space to stop if the vehicle in front brakes or changes course. Rear-end collisions are caused by not paying attention or by following too closely.

15. In slow-moving traffic, you may need to reduce the distance between you and the car ahead to maintain traffic flow. However, don't get so close that you can't stop safely. If the traffic is blocked, always leave just enough space to manoeuvre should the vehicle in front break down or an emergency services vehicle need to get past.

16. In narrow residential streets with parked cars you shouldn't normally exceed 20 mph. Look out for hazards such as
• vehicles emerging from junctions
• vehicles moving off
• car doors opening
• pedestrians running out from between parked cars

17. If you are in a line of slow-moving traffic, don't stop directly on a pedestrian crossing. Try to judge the flow of traffic and leave a gap for pedestrians to cross.

ROAD USERS YOU SHOULD BE PARTICULARLY AWARE OF

Pedestrians

18. In urban areas there is a high risk of pedestrians – especially children – stepping unexpectedly into the road. At 40 mph your vehicle will probably kill any pedestrian it hits. At 20 mph there is a 1 in 20 chance of the pedestrian being killed. So kill your speed.

19. Elderly pedestrians may need more time to cross the road. Be patient and allow them to cross in their own time. Don't hurry them by waving at them or revving the engine.

20. If you need to reverse into a side road, look all around the vehicle and give way to any pedestrians who may be crossing the road.

Cyclists

21. Take care when you pass cyclists. Be prepared for cyclists to go in any direction at road junctions or roundabouts. They are slow and vulnerable and it is often safer for them to stay in the near-side lane even when they are going most of the way round a roundabout.

Elderly drivers

22. The reactions of elderly drivers may not be quite as fast as they once were. Make allowance for this.

Inexperienced drivers

23. You should also be prepared for drivers who may have little driving experience and whose reactions may not be quite as fast as those of a more practised driver. Most young drivers are relatively inexperienced. Be particularly patient with learner drivers.

Lorries and other large vehicles

24. Large vehicles can block your view. Dropping back may increase your ability to see and to plan ahead.

25. If you plan to overtake a large vehicle, keep well back to get the best view of the road ahead. Passing a large vehicle is more risky and can take a long time because of its length. Make sure that you have room to complete your overtaking before you commit yourself. Don't take risks. If in doubt, don't overtake.

26. If the vehicle ahead begins to overtake a large or long vehicle, don't assume that you can follow it. If a problem develops, the vehicle ahead may abort overtaking and need to drop back.

27. A large vehicle may need extra road space to turn or to deal with a hazard that you aren't able to see. If you are following a large vehicle – an articulated lorry, for instance – be prepared to stop and wait if it needs room or time to turn.

Motorcycles

28. If you are following a motorcycle, be prepared for it to swerve. You may not be able to see what lies ahead. Motorcyclists may need to avoid uneven road surfaces in wet weather such as drain covers and other road features.

Buses, coaches, trams, electric vehicles and ice cream vans

29. Look out for people getting on and off buses, coaches and trams. Be particularly attentive if you are passing a school bus or an ice cream van, as children may run out from behind it.

30. Be careful of electric vehicles. Trams move quickly and silently and are unable to steer to avoid you.

Animals

31. In the country you are more likely to find animals in the road. If a road is blocked by a herd of animals, stop and switch off your engine until they have left the road.

32. Be particularly careful with groups of horses and riders – some of the riders may be learners.

MAKING SURE THAT YOU ARE FIT TO DRIVE

Don't drive if you feel unwell or are taking drugs which may affect your driving. If in doubt about the effect of medicinal drugs, don't drive.

33. Check the instructions on medicines to make sure that they don't affect your driving. If in doubt, ask your doctor.

34. If you feel tired or sleepy while driving, pull over into a safe place (not the hard shoulder of a motorway) and take a short rest. Some exercise or coffee while you stop will help to keep you alert and improve your concentration.

35. Make sure that you dress appropriately for driving. You should be comfortable, and what you wear shouldn't interfere with your control of the vehicle. Suitable shoes are particularly important to ensure that you can use the pedals safely.

HANDLING YOUR VEHICLE CORRECTLY

Make sure that you can use the controls and equipment of your vehicle correctly.

Before setting off

36. Adjust your seat and mirrors to ensure comfort, full control and maximum vision. Properly adjusted head restraints will reduce the risk of neck injuries in the event of an accident.

General

37. Remain in full control of the vehicle at all times. Leaning your arm on the door, resting your hand on the gear-stick or handbrake, or holding the steering wheel with only one hand makes it harder to regain full control if an unexpected hazard arises.

38. Make sure that you never run out of petrol. It can be very dangerous to lose power when driving in traffic. Only carry petrol in a can or tank designed for that purpose.

Braking and acceleration

39. Except in an emergency, the safest way to brake is to brake lightly, then harder as you begin to stop, then ease off just before stopping. Easing the pressure as the car comes to rest avoids a jerky stop.

40. In an emergency, brake immediately. If your vehicle isn't fitted with anti-lock brakes (ABS), try to avoid locking your wheels by using 'cadence braking'. (See paragraph 41.)

41. If the vehicle begins to skid when braking on a wet or slippery road, release the brake pedal to allow the wheels to turn and then brake again more gently. This may be repeated many times and is known as 'cadence braking'.

42. Anti-lock braking systems apply cadence braking automatically without the need to release the brake pedal so you shouldn't apply this technique if your vehicle has ABS. If your vehicle is fitted with ABS you should continue to push hard on the pedal. ABS will prevent the wheels from locking and so enable you to steer around an obstacle.

43. Heavy acceleration, fast driving and late or harsh braking all increase fuel consumption. Use fuel economically.

44. Water on brakes may cause them to lose their effectiveness. If you have driven through water – for instance a flood, burst main or a ford – test your brakes at the first safe opportunity by pushing gently on the brake pedal, to make sure that they work. If they don't work, continue to apply the brakes gently while driving slowly. This will help to dry them out.

Coasting

45. Don't coast whatever the driving conditions. Coasting occurs when you allow your vehicle to travel in neutral or with the clutch depressed. This reduces the driver's control of the vehicle as it eliminates the effect of engine braking. This means you have to use the footbrake more, and over-use can reduce its effectiveness. Coasting can also reduce steering control on bends and corners, increase vehicle speed on hills, and make it more difficult to select the appropriate gear when you need it.

Turning and reversing

46. When turning or reversing you should check all round for other road users or pedestrians. Use your mirrors but look mainly through the rear and side windows.

Lights and signals

47. Think about the signals you give to other road users. Make sure that your use of indicators won't mislead others. If, for instance, you want to stop after a side road, avoid signalling too early or it may give the impression that you intend to turn into the road. Use indicators even if there are no other vehicles, for the benefit of pedestrians.

48. If you think that your indicators can't be seen clearly because another driver's view is obstructed, use an arm signal as well to emphasise the point.

49. If an emergency services vehicle following you flashes its headlights, allow it to overtake when it is safe to do so.

On hills

50. To help control your speed on a long downhill slope, slow down and select a low gear before you reach the slope. Use the brakes carefully.

51. If you park on a hill, apply the handbrake firmly. Turning the front wheels so they face into the kerb will help to stop the car rolling downhill. Leave the car in gear – a forward gear if pointing uphill and reverse if pointing downhill. Use 'park' if your car has an automatic gearbox.

DRIVING IN BAD WEATHER

Try to avoid driving in bad weather. If you must drive, take particular care. Drive only at a speed which allows you to stop within the distance you can see to be clear.

In wet weather

- Stopping distances will be up to four times greater than on dry roads because your tyres have less grip on the road. Keep well back from the vehicle in front. This will increase your ability to see and plan ahead.
- The steering may be affected. If you are driving on wet roads and the steering becomes light, it means that the water is preventing the tyres from gripping the road.

Ease off the accelerator and slow down gradually if this happens.
- Spray from large vehicles may make it difficult to see so use dipped headlights.

52. In icy or snowy weather

- Before starting your journey, clear snow and ice from the windows, mirrors, lights and number plates of your vehicle. Make sure the windows are de-misted thoroughly.
- Stopping distances can be ten times greater than on dry roads, so keep well behind the vehicle in front.
- Be extra gentle on the controls when the roads are icy as any sudden movement could cause you to skid. Drive at a slow speed in as high a gear as possible with low revs to avoid wheelspin.
- When approaching bends and hazards, brake well before you reach the bend and try to brake only when travelling in a straight line. Otherwise you might skid. Slow right down before turning and steer smoothly, avoiding sudden movements.
- Check your grip on the road surface when there is snow or ice by choosing a safe place to brake gently. If the steering feels light, this may indicate black ice and your vehicle losing its grip on the road.

Skids

53. Don't think you can fully control a skid – there is rarely enough space.

54. Avoid anything which may cause a skid, but if you do lose control, steer in the direction of the skid. For instance, if the rear skids to the right, steer quickly and smoothly to the right to recover.

55. In windy weather

- Cars are less likely to be affected by strong winds than high-sided vehicles, but remember that it is still possible for strong gusts to blow a car off-course.
- Open stretches of road can often be exposed to strong cross-winds. Look out for gaps in hedges or bridges which may alter the effects of the wind on your vehicle.

- If it is very windy, you may be affected by windbreaks or eddies created by passing large vehicles.
- Take extra care when passing pedal and motorcyclists who can be blown off-course by the wind. Keep well back from a cyclist overtaking a high-sided vehicle.

56. In fog or poor visibility

- Slow down, because you can't see events ahead.
- At junctions with limited visibility, stop in the correct position and then move forward carefully, checking both ways as fully as possible. When you are sure it is safe to emerge, do so decisively. Once you have reached a position where you would be in the path of approaching traffic, don't stop.
- Keep well back from the vehicle ahead in case it stops suddenly. This is particularly important when travelling fast on motorways and dual carriageways, when vehicles can unexpectedly enter fog banks.

57. In very hot weather

Be careful if the road surface becomes soft. Your steering and braking might be affected.

DRIVING AT NIGHT

Driving at night is more dangerous than driving in daylight, so be particularly alert. You can see less detail and might not see bends in the road and other hazards.

58. Use your lights thoughtfully. When overtaking, remain on dipped headlights until you are level with the other vehicle and then change to main beam. This enables both cars to see ahead. If a vehicle approaches from the other direction, or you are behind another vehicle, dip your lights. Dazzling other drivers is dangerous.

59. If you have left a brightly lit building, give your eyes time to adjust before driving. If your night vision is poor, don't drive.

DRIVING ON MOTORWAYS AND DUAL CARRIAGEWAYS

Motorways are generally safer than other roads. When accidents do happen they can be very severe, due to the speed of the traffic.

After you have passed your practical test it is advisable to take some lessons on the motorway before you drive unsupervised.

60. Before you start your journey, make sure that you and your vehicle can cope with the demands of high-speed driving. Check your vehicle's
• oil
• water
• tyres
Doing this will reduce the risk of a breakdown.

61. Always keep to the left lane unless overtaking. This applies whatever speed you are travelling at. Even at 70 mph on a motorway you should drive in the left lane if the road ahead is clear.

62. Check your mirrors carefully before overtaking or changing lanes. If you want to change into another lane, wait until it is clear before indicating.

63. Large vehicles aren't allowed to use the outside lane of a motorway which has three or more lanes. Thoughtless driving can impede their progress.

64. Contraflow systems on motorways mean that you are travelling in a narrower lane than normal and with no permanent barrier between you and traffic coming towards you. You are twice as likely to have an accident on a two-way contraflow compared to normal driving. Drive slowly and keep a good distance from the vehicle ahead, observing any speed limits.

VEHICLE DEFECTS AND SAFETY EQUIPMENT

65. Make sure that you understand the meaning of all warning displays on the instrument panel. Don't ignore warning signs of faults developing. Your safety and that of others may be put at risk.

66. Warning lights for brakes – fluid level warning, brake pad wear, anti-lock brakes (ABS) and the parking brake (handbrake) – should light up and then go out again when the vehicle moves off. If they don't, a dangerous fault may have developed and you shouldn't drive the vehicle before having checks made.

67. If the warning lights for oil or water temperature come on while you are driving, stop and have the problem investigated immediately. There may be a serious fault which could lead to engine seizure.

68. If the charge warning light comes on while you are driving, it may mean that the battery isn't charging. This must also be checked as soon as possible to avoid loss of power for lights and other electrical systems.

69. Make sure that you know where the switch for the hazard warning lights is located. Both the switch and the warning light are red and marked with a triangle.

70. Check tyre pressures at frequent intervals. Do this before your journey, when they are cold. Warm or hot tyres may give a misleading reading. Your braking and steering will be adversely affected by under-inflated or over-inflated tyres.

71. Excessive or uneven tyre wear may be caused by faults in the braking or suspension systems, or wheels which are out of alignment. Have these faults corrected as soon as possible.

72. If your vehicle pulls to one side when braking, it is most likely to be caused by poorly adjusted brakes. However, incorrectly inflated tyres or a serious mechanical failure may also be the problem. Consult a garage or mechanic immediately.

73. If a vehicle continues to bounce after pushing down on the front or rear, its shock absorbers are worn. Worn shock absorbers can seriously affect the operation of a vehicle and must be replaced.

74. Ensure that unusual smells are investigated immediately. Burning rubber, electrical or petrol smells need urgent checks. Don't risk a fire.

75. Check the fluid levels in your vehicle frequently. Low brake fluid may result in brake failure and an accident. Make sure you recognise the low fluid warning lights if your vehicle has them.

76. In petrol stations, never smoke on the forecourt. This is hazardous and is a major fire risk.

77. If your car has additional lights which aren't required by law, they must be correctly fitted and adjusted and in working order.

78. It is advisable to use child locks if you carry children in the back seats. Child locks prevent the rear doors being opened from the inside.

DOCUMENTS NEEDED TO DRIVE

Always make sure that you have the correct documents for driving. You don't have to carry most documents with you, but you must be able to produce your driving licence, a valid insurance certificate and – where appropriate – a valid MOT certificate at a police station within seven days, if you are asked to do so by a police officer.

Driving licence

79. You must have a valid driving licence for the category of vehicle you are driving. Remember that driving licences aren't valid until signed.

Insurance

80. You must not drive an uninsured motor vehicle. You must at least have cover for risks to third parties. Before driving any vehicle, check that it has this cover for your use or that your own insurance policy covers you.

81.   If you are involved in an accident, you should give your name and address and details of your insurance to anyone who has been injured or whose vehicle or property has been or may have been damaged. You should also give these details to anyone else having reasonable cause to need it, such as a police officer.

MOT

82.   Cars and motorcycles must pass an MOT test three years from the date of first registration and every year after that. Make sure that any vehicle you drive has a valid MOT certificate if it needs one. Driving a vehicle without an MOT certificate is illegal, potentially dangerous and can invalidate your insurance.

83.   The only time that you may drive a vehicle on the road without an MOT certificate is when driving to a pre-arranged test appointment or to a garage for repairs required for the test.

84.   An MOT certificate only shows the condition of the vehicle at the time of the test. If a defect develops after the test, you must have it put right.

Vehicle registration document

85.   All vehicles used on the road must have a registration document giving details of the registered owner, the make of vehicle, the type of body and its engine type and size. If you buy a car, make sure that the Driver & Vehicle Licensing Agency is notified so that a new document can be issued to you.

Vehicle excise duty

86.   All vehicles used or kept on the roads must have a valid Vehicle Excise Duty disc (tax disc) displayed on the windscreen (or elsewhere for motorcycles) at all times. A new disc can normally be purchased from a post office. To do so, you will need the vehicle registration document (or the reminder issued by the Driver & Vehicle Licensing Agency), a valid insurance certificate and, where appropriate, a valid MOT certificate.

BREAKDOWNS AND ACCIDENT HANDLING

87. If you have a flat tyre, stop as soon as it is safe to do so. Only change the tyre if you can do so without putting yourself or others at risk – otherwise call a breakdown service.

88. If a tyre bursts while you are driving, try to keep control of your vehicle. Grip the steering wheel firmly and allow the vehicle to roll to a stop at the side of the road.

89. Most engines are water cooled. If your engine overheats, wait until it has cooled naturally. Only then remove the coolant filler cap and add water or coolant.

90. If your vehicle catches fire, get the occupants out of the vehicle quickly and to a safe place. Don't attempt to extinguish a fire in the engine compartment, as opening the bonnet will make the fire flare up. Call the fire brigade.

91. It is advisable to carry a first aid kit in case you are involved in or arrive at the scene of an accident.

92. Pages 75 and 76 explain what to do at the scene of an accident. Keep injured people calm by talking to them. Keep them warm and comfortable. Don't leave an injured person unattended.

VEHICLE LOADING

93. As a driver, you are responsible for making sure that your vehicle or trailer is not overloaded. You should load a trailer or caravan so that the weight is evenly distributed. This will help to prevent it swerving, snaking or going out of control. If your trailer or caravan begins to swerve or snake, ease off the accelerator and reduce speed gently.